to the

Prodigal Bride

(based on the Song of Solomon)

Be Blessed in His Wonderful Love,
Gerry

by

Gerry Isaacs Harris

The Song To The Prodigal Bride

Published by:

Serenity Books
P.O. Box 3595
Hagerstown, MD 21742-3595

ISBN 1-884369-46-4

Printed in the United States of America
For Worldwide Distribution

Return,

return,

O

Shulamite,

return,

return!

Dedication

I would like to dedicate this book to our son Dan, whose direction and encouragement really inspired me to pursue a dream and not give up, until it became a reality. Than you, Dan.

Acknowledgments

I wish to thank our daughter Kim and her family for supporting me through their prayers. Also, thank you, Kim, Jennifer and Ben, for helping me to get started on my computer.

I also wish to thank our son Jim and his family and my sister Merldean and brother Robert for their prayers and encouragement.

Thank you to my friends, Christine, Ginny, Sheila, Tziporah, Elaine and Betty, who shared my search and who have supported me through their prayers and words of loving encouragement. Elaine, how can I thank you enough for the sacrificial time and effort you spent proofreading my text, and for your very helpful suggestions?

A "special thanks" to Kay, who began the typing of my manuscript and who helped me in countless other ways. You were such an encouragement!

Last, but certainly not least, I wish to thank my husband, Lowell, who generously allowed me to spend much time "apart" in my seeking and in my endeavors — always being there as a listener and support. Thank you for your words of wisdom and your loving encouragement to me. I believe that our relationship grew even sweeter and stronger during my writing about our relationship with our Heavenly Bridegroom. (I am writing this on the anniversary of our 40th year of marriage.)

Author's Foreword

I would never have thought that I would be even attempting to write a book. But what I have written is more a sharing of my heart with a desire that others would look more deeply into God's love song, "Song of Solomon," or "Song of Songs," as it is called in the original Hebrew text, and find the blessing that I have found in letting this book speak to my heart. This is my prayer, as I have attempted to put my thoughts onto paper.

As you read it, may God's great love "draw you." May His sweetness fill you with ecstasy and strength and cause you to become all that He desires for His Bride to be in Him. And may we, together, bring Him glory and blessing with our lives, hidden in Him.

Introduction

In a time of deep personal grief, I sensed the Holy Spirit telling me to read the Song of Solomon. This was definitely a new experience for me, but I was obedient and opened the book to read. In previous attempts, which had not been recent or many, I had not been able to gain much insight or understanding from this book which seemed to me to be speaking primarily about the marriage relationship.

As I read and reread the book, several verses seemed to stand out as not fitting into the context of the book and I puzzled over them trying to "see" what meaning they held. I went to our senior pastor and shared these thoughts with him, asking him for any help he might be able to give me. He seemed as puzzled over them as I was.

A few days later I shared these experiences with a small group of ladies in a Bible study. One of them told me that she had a book, written by Watchman Nee, called the *Song of Songs* and would be happy to let me read it. Mr. Nee's book was a tremendous help in "unlocking" the Song of Songs to me, as in it the author explained that the Song was written as an allegory and offered help in interpreting some of the symbolic meanings. How precious it was as I began to see that this book was a love song being sung to *me* by my "King!"

This caused me to desire all the more to understand these verses which still remained a "mystery" to me, hidden from my comprehension. I searched for other books written on the Song of Solomon, hoping to gain further insights from these, but was not able to obtain much help from them either.

Sharing these blessings, and desires, with the friend who had lent me her book caused her and another friend to ask if we might "look into" this book together. We did. A small group of women joined us in doing a verse-by-verse searching and sharing. We looked up many of the words of the book in *Strong's Concordance* to learn the original meaning of the Hebrew text and gained much help through this. Other groups asked if I would lead them through the study, and our pastor asked me to lead a group during our church's Wednesday night Bible study. Several people began to tell me that they were finding greater intimacy in their relationship with God and that their lives were being changed through "listening to the Love Song."

I'm not sure, whether or not, that I yet know the meaning of these "mysterious" verses, but I do know that my life has been greatly changed by my search. One of these verses was: *"Before I was even aware, my soul had made me as the chariots of my noble people."* One day it dawned upon me that this verse had come to pass in my own life. I had been changed, as His Bride, from *"my filly among*

Pharaoh's chariots" into *"a chariot of my noble people,"* as I had been drawn in my heart to pray for and to financially support the return of the Jewish people to their homeland, Israel. It also seemed to me that God had brought some precious Jewish people into my life that He wanted me to comfort (Song of Solomon 6:12 and 1:9 and Isaiah 40:1,2).

But the change inside me had gone deeper than this, for the Bible now seemed more like "one" book to me. It also became even more personal to me as I now began to see myself as a part of the fulfillment of the prophecies concerning Israel. If I had become a part of His bride, then surely the prophecies concerning Israel included me. If God is One, and He declares that He is, surely He has only one bride. Many say that the church became "spiritual Israel," but the "new covenant" that God promised to make was with the house of Israel and with the house of Judah. Also, the promise of forgiveness of sin was usually followed by a promise to return them to the land. How can we take one part of the promise — *"For I will forgive their iniquity and their sin I will remember no more"* (Jeremiah 31:34 and 33:7-8) — and leave the rest? — *"On the day that I cleanse you from all your iniquities, I will also enable you to dwell in the cities and the ruins shall be rebuilt"* (Ezekiel 36:33)? How can we take His promise of spiritual blessing and refuse His promise of physical blessing?

As I diligently sought for the answers to these questions, I am not sure whether my search produced more answers or questions. Probably more questions. My desire, therefore, in writing this book is definitely not to propagate a new doctrine, but my hope is that as you read the words of this book, your thinking will also be challenged, and that it will cause you to look again, deeply, into the Word of God.

Most of all, I pray that you will also be encouraged to let the richness of His great love fill your heart, and melt every barrier of resistance within you. I pray that each of us will answer His call, *"Return, return, O Shulamite; return, return,"* whatever that may mean in each of our own lives. I pray that, through His Love Song, each of us will be drawn and transformed into His holy Bride without spot, wrinkle or blemish.

I have written this book in the first person, except in the narration following the first verse of the text, even as the Song of Songs is written in the first person. I have done this because I believe that we are to enter into it as His bride, and receive all the words of this "Love Song" as though they were being sung to us, personally; for they are! Then, I believe that He desires us to respond to Him in the same personal way. As we "run with Him" (and with the rest of the Bride), we will be drawn closer to Him. We will grow in our love for Him and in our understanding of His ways. We will find that sin and lusts hold less and less power over us. We will be prepared, as His Bride, to rule and reign with Him in His Kingdom.

Gerry Harris
Traverse City, Michigan

Draw me
we will run after thee

Chapter One

The song of songs, which is Solomon's.
                                    Song of Songs 1:1

"The Song," which is not heard by the ears, but by the heart, is sung by the Bridegroom King to His Bride — ever awakening love within her and causing her to desire to be drawn nearer to Him.

"The Song" brought us to Him in the first place — as through it we heard of this great Creator King who formed us by His own hands. Then, because of His great love for us, He took on the form of flesh and, at the hands of those He created, became the sacrifice that would cleanse and restore His Bride to Him.

"The Song" stirred our hearts to believe that the love which He poured out by His death on the cross was even for us, that we could be "one who was called" to Him. We could be loved by Him! We could become part of His Bride!

"His Song" of total love and acceptance, when we came to him clad in filthy rags, totally unworthy of a king's court, empty, with nothing to offer, ignorant of what it would mean to become the bride of a king, quickly washed away our self doubts. We could only marvel at His love for us.

"The Song" brought us into a place of such richness, security, and fulfillment that our past life seemed "far removed," and we were thrilled by the new life we were given as His Bride. We were clothed in beautiful garments of righteousness and fed with His words, which were as honey and wine to us — giving us strength and joy. He replaced our "old life" with such beautiful new abundant life that we knew we could never leave Him or turn back.

Through "the Song," our Bridegroom called us to come with Him to heights that our own strength could never reach, to places where we were fearful of following, and where only the power of His Love Song could bring us.

But as we are drawn by "the Song" and follow after our Bridegroom King, we find ourselves being transformed by it, our hearts being melted by His consummate love, so that our joy and fulfillment come only in following Him. Wherever it may lead us, we must follow "the Song" and be brought nearer and nearer to Him, "the Singer," Who has consumed our heart by His Love Song.

"The Song" drew us along the pathway that led from the beginning of the relationship — the place of our meeting Him and receiving His love — to a place of growth and maturity, a place of our willingness to lay down our own lives for our brother, even as He had laid His down for us.

"The Song" brings prophetic revelation to us, His

Bride, as, through "the Song," our veil is lifted and we are given "new vision," even light for our path that will lead us toward our new home — where we will live forever as the Bride of this King of Peace in His City of Peace.

Also I saw the holy city, New Yerushalayim [Jerusalem], coming down out of heaven from God, prepared like a bride beautifully dressed for her husband. Revelation 21:2 (JNT)

Let Him kiss me with the kisses of His mouth — For your love is better than wine. Song of Songs 1:2

After hearing the words of His "Love Song" and seeing the beauty of "the Singer," longing and desire rise up within me. I want to receive more than words written on a page. In these words I see His greatness, His wisdom, and His power. But I desire more than this. I want to hear His voice singing His "Love Song" to *me*. I want to know Him intimately!

I find myself crying out, "Sing Your Love Song to me, for it is intoxicating. It warms me and fills me with desire for You! It lifts me up above the cares of this world and causes me to glimpse a realm I've never seen before. It fills me with joy and anticipation. There is nothing to compare with the sweetness of Your love. It is much better than wine! Much more uplifting and much longer lasting than anything that the world can offer me!"

You are fairer than the sons of men; Grace is poured upon Your lips; therefore God has blessed you forever. Psalm 45:2

Because of the fragrance of Your good ointments, Your name is ointment poured forth; Therefore the virgins love you.
Song of Songs 1:3

I sing out in response to His Song: "The precious words of Your Love Song are anointed to call forth Your Bride. They are as a fragrance that draws me and causes me to desire You. Their sweetness is greater than any I have ever sensed. Your Name, given to You by Your Father, carries an anointing. It contains all power and authority — It is the Name above all names! Yet, through the power of Your love, You completely emptied Yourself, and every drop of Your power was poured out — totally given, freely given, lovingly given — that You might receive us, wash us, heal us, clothe us, renew us, restore us; that we might be fully prepared and brought to You as Your Bride. This is love — far greater than any love I have ever known, greater than any love I have ever experienced, greater than any love I have ever heard about. It is beyond my comprehension! But, because of it, I cannot help but love You too!

"Could it be that I could come to You? That I could actually become a part of Your Kingdom? That I could become Your Bride?"

For unto us a Child is born, unto us a Son is given; and the government will be upon His shoulder, and His name will be called Wonderful, Counselor, Mighty God, Everlasting Father, Prince of Peace. Of the increase of His government and peace there will be no end, upon the throne of David and over His kingdom, to order it and establish it with judgment and justice from that time forward, even forever. The zeal of the LORD of hosts will perform this. Isaiah 9:6-7

Therefore the Lord Himself will give you a sign: Behold, the virgin shall conceive and bear a Son, and shall call His name Immanuel. Isaiah 7:14

Now in the sixth month the angel Gabriel was sent by God to a city of Galilee named

Nazareth, to a virgin betrothed to a man whose name was Joseph, of the house of David. The virgin's name was Mary. ... "And behold, you will conceive in your womb and bring forth a Son, and shall call His name JESUS [Yeshua]. He will be great, and will be called the Son of the Highest; and the Lord God will give Him the throne of His father David. And He will reign over the house of Jacob forever, and of His kingdom there will be no end."

Luke 1:26-27 & 31-33

The Spirit of the Lord GOD is upon Me, because the LORD has anointed Me to preach good tidings to the poor; He has sent Me to heal the brokenhearted, to proclaim liberty to the captives, and the opening of the prison to those who are bound; to proclaim the acceptable year of the LORD. Isaiah 61:1-2

Therefore God raised Him to the highest place and gave him the name above every name; that in honor of the name given Yeshua, every knee will bow — in heaven, on earth and under the earth — and every tongue will acknowledge that Yeshua [Jesus] the Messiah [Christ] is Adonai [LORD] to the glory of God the Father. Philippians 2:9-11 (JNT)

AUTHOR'S NOTE: His name, *Yeshua*, meaning salvation, or saviour, was spoken long before He was born through the prophets that *heard* His name and said that He would come — this Prince of Peace, Emmanuel (God with us), Everlasting Father, Mighty God. The angel, Gabriel, spoke His name to the virgin as he told her that she would conceive Him, announcing that He would be anointed to sit on the throne of His forefather, David — ushering in the kingdom that would know no end!

Lead me away! [Draw me, KJV] We will run after you. The king has brought me into his chambers! We will be glad and rejoice in you. We will remember your love more than wine. Rightly do they love you.
Song of Songs 1:4

As I hear "the Song," my heart is filled with longing to be able to come to this One who is so lovely in every way. Pride and self-consciousness give way to desire and I find myself crying out from the depths of my being, "Choose me — call me — let me be one who is brought to You — chosen to be one of the company who follows after You. I will follow You gladly if You will only call me to Yourself."

I have no idea what this will mean in my life or where it will take me, but the words seemed to just rise up out of the depths of me as my heart responds to the "kisses of His lips," the loving words He has spoken — offering Himself to all who would come to Him. What more could I offer to Him in response to His great gift of love?

It seems that the words are hardly out of my mouth until I know that He has answered my cry. It is as though everything had changed. I know that He has received me. I feel like a new person! I feel washed, clean, made new! I feel so loved, fully accepted, completely received — by One who is so beautiful, so awesome, so wonderful! I sense His great love for me and that He is nearer than any friend or lover I've ever had. I feel that His desire to draw me near to Him is as great, or greater, than even my own desire to be called. I sense His pleasure in receiving me, and I am amazed. My heart overflows with joy as I sing out, together, with the others He has drawn: "We rejoice in Your goodness and love for us, Mighty King!" Another group responds, as if a part of the refrain, "We remember all Your goodness and love to us in the past." And we join together singing, "Rightly do they love You, oh Mighty One! For You are worthy of all our praise."

And yet, it is amazing how personal and intimate His love seems to me — as though I were one alone, instead of one of a company!

I drew them with gentle cords [cords of a man, marginal note in NKJ], with bands of

*love, and I was to them as those who take the
yoke from their neck. I stooped and fed them.*
Hosea 11:4

*Incline your ear, and come to Me. Hear, and
your soul shall live; And I will make an everlasting covenant with you— The sure mercies
of David. Indeed I have given him as a witness
to the people, a leader and commander for the
people. Surely you shall call a nation you do
not know, and nations who do not know you
shall run to you, because of the LORD your
God and the Holy One of Israel; for He has glorified you.* Isaiah 55:3-5

*And I, if I am lifted up from the earth, will
draw all peoples to Myself.* John 12:32

AUTHOR'S NOTE: *Draw me,* the words used in the
King James Version, have a variety of meanings
in the original Hebrew, including "to sow, to
sound [as by voice], to prolong, to develop, to
march, to delay — draw (along, out) continue,
forbear, etc." (*Strongs Exhaustive Concordance*
#4900)

I could never have guessed that day when I
prayed, "Draw me," where His love would lead
me. "Draw me," when prayed from the heart, is
one of the most powerful prayers we can pray.
As we begin to hear "His voice," the voice of
His Spirit within us, and we dare to follow, we

21

will be led on paths that we would never have dreamed of when we were choosing our own way. It is a pathway of joy, adventure, tears and sometimes suffering. But, if we dare to follow, He always leads us nearer to Himself and nearer to the goal that He has set for us. His desire is to form us into His Bride without spot and blemish — radiating His love. It is a powerful prayer. Will we dare to pray it often? Will we dare to follow Him when He calls? And will we faithfully follow Him to the end?

I am dark [black, KJV], but lovely, O daughters of Jerusalem, like the tents of Kedar, like the curtains of Solomon.
Song of Songs 1:5

All at once I become aware that I am being scrutinized by the ones who have walked longer with Him as His Bride. Not sensing their approval of me, I become self-conscious, realizing that, though I have been cleansed and made new in my spirit, my outward appearance has not been changed. All that the onlookers can see is that I am dressed in the clothing of the nations where I have wandered, and that I have taken on their manner of speech and their customs.

In my discomfort, I begin to defend myself before them, saying, "Please don't judge me as an outsider because of my appearance, nor even by my speech or behavior. For the King has called me and He has brought me into His kingdom. I am beautiful in His eyes!"

✡   ✡   ✡

The people who walked in darkness have seen a great light; those who dwelt in the land of the shadow of death, upon them a light has shined. You have multiplied the nation and increased its joy. ... For unto us a Child is born, unto us a Son is given. ... Of the increase of His government and peace, there will be no end, upon the throne of David and over His kingdom, to order it and establish it with judgment and justice from that time forward, even forever. The zeal of the LORD of hosts will perform this.   Isaiah 9:2-3 & 6-7

He will be as a sanctuary, but a stone of stumbling and a rock of offense to both the houses of Israel, as a trap and a snare to the inhabitants of Jerusalem.   Isaiah 8:14

AUTHOR'S NOTE: In the original Hebrew text, the word *black* is taken from a root which can also mean "to dawn, to be up early, seeking or inquiring." It seems to give the indication that the Bride is at the beginning of her "rebirth," and that though she has been fully cleansed and accepted by her Lover, she still has much to learn and to experience. Though fully accepted, she

23

still has need of growth in learning how to walk in the ways of His kingdom.

There also seems to be a possible allusion to the Bride being taken from the nations, as referred to here by "the curtains of Solomon," which provided the intimate chambers where King Solomon came into union with his many wives and concubines. Even so, our Heavenly Bridegroom has "called" us from all the nations of the earth to come into His courts and become His Bride.

Do not look upon me, because I am dark [black, KJV], because the sun has tanned me. My mother's sons were angry with me; They made me the keeper of the vineyards, but my own vineyard I have not kept. Song of Songs 1:6

I try to excuse my appearance to them by reminding them, "Even from generations past I have been despised and rejected by my family. It was even because of their jealous acts that I was not allowed to remain at home to watch over our father's vineyard. Instead, I became the keeper of other vineyards after I was 'cast out.' I know that in your eyes I still do not measure up and that, as yet, you do not find me acceptable to walk with the King and become part of His Kingdom."

✿　✿　✿

AUTHOR'S NOTE: There are at least two instances, recorded in Scripture, where the brothers, *mother's sons*, became angry. One is the brothers of Joseph. Because of the "favour" given him by his father, demonstrated by his gift of the coat made of many colors, his brothers became jealous of him. They, therefore, cast him away from themselves by selling him as a slave to a band of Ishmaelites who were taking slaves down to Egypt to sell them there. He was not allowed to keep his father's vineyard but kept the Pharaoh's vineyard instead. He was not even recognized by his brothers when they saw him again.

Another instance of the brothers becoming angry was when the Gentiles began to become part of the house of Israel by being taken into the congregation through receiving Yeshua as the Messiah. Most of them knew almost nothing of "Torah," the law. They were not trained in the traditions and lifestyle of the Jews. They were filled with pagan ways. Therefore, they seemed "black" (unclean and unacceptable) because of their pagan customs, and were not received by many of the Jews at that time.

The blessing spoken over Joseph by his father, Jacob, just before his death, was that he would be a fruitful bough whose branches would run over the wall. He also spoke to Joseph that the shepherd, the stone of Israel would be from thence:

Joseph is a fruitful bough, a fruitful bough by a well; his branches run over the wall. The archers have bitterly grieved him, shot at him and hated him. But his bow remained in strength and the arms of his hands were made strong by the hands of the Mighty God of Jacob (From there is the Shepherd, the Stone of Israel), by the God of your father who will help you, and by the Almighty who will bless you with blessings of heaven above, blessings of the deep that lies beneath, blessings of the breasts and of the womb. The blessings of your father have excelled the blessings of my ancestors, up to the utmost bound of the everlasting hills. They shall be on the head of Joseph, and on the crown of the head of him who was separate from his brothers. Genesis 49:22-26

Hear the word of the Lord, you who tremble at His word; "Your brethren who hated you cast you out for My name's sake said: 'Let the Lord be glorified, that we may see your joy,' but they shall be ashamed." Isaiah 66:5

But the Jerusalem above is free, which is the mother of us all. Galatians 4:26

Is it possible that the descendants of Joseph, which later became the northern kingdom, referred to as "Ephraim" or "Israel," which was *cut off,* are being regathered (re-grafted) in the Messiah Yeshua?

Tell me, O you whom I love, Where you feed your flock, where you make it rest at noon, For why should I be as one who veils herself by the flock of your companions?   Song of Songs 1:7

I come to Him knowing that I am fully accepted by Him as His Bride, yet before the others I feel insecure, uneducated, and inexperienced in the ways of His kingdom. I become painfully aware of my ignorance. In my immaturity and impatience I ask, "Where do I receive the help and teaching that I need to learn the ways of Your kingdom? Why can't You just instruct me and tell me all that I need to know concerning Your plans for Your kingdom *now*? Why should I be looked upon as unworthy? Why must I suffer their rejection? Why must my identity be kept hidden? Why can't You just reveal me as Your Bride to the rest of Your companions *now*?"

I ask for a full revelation, "Where do we rest at noon?" Yet He is not ready to reveal these things to me, His "newborn" Bride. He is not so much interested in giving me answers that He knows I am not ready to receive. Rather, He desires that I grow in my relationship to Him, first, and then to the rest of the "family" (flock).

Knowledge will be given gradually as I receive and learn to walk in the "light" that I have already been given. It will grow and increase as I walk along with Him.

But the path of the just is like the shining sun, that shines ever brighter unto the perfect day.
Proverbs 4:18

For, brothers, I want you to understand this truth which God formerly concealed but has now revealed, so that you won't imagine you know more than you actually do. It is that stoniness, to a degree, has come upon Israel, until the Gentile world enters in its fullness; and that it is in this way that all Israel will be saved. As the Tanakh says, "Out of Tziyon will come the Redeemer; he will turn away ungodliness from Ya'akov [Jacob] and this will be my covenant with them, ... when I take away their sins." Romans 11:25-27 (JNT)
(From Isaiah 59:20-21, 27:9
& Jeremiah 31:33-34)

AUTHOR'S NOTE: In the King James Version the words *turneth aside* (instead of *veiled*, as in the text above) are used. These words in Hebrew seem to contain the possible meaning of "ap-pearing," "(re-)turning" after being 'cast out.' *Aside* can mean "being wrapped or hidden," as "turned aside." (SC #6437 and #5844) The Bride's desire to be seen by others in her new relationship to the King, is similar to Joseph's when he wore his coat, showing that he had been favored by his father. He caused anger and jealousy in his brothers by wearing his coat in their presence and also by telling them of his dreams of being *lifted to greatness* above them.

If you do not know, O fairest among women, follow in the footsteps of the flock, and feed your little goats beside the shepherd's tents.   Song of Songs 1:8

"If you don't, as yet, have full knowledge of the ways of My kingdom and of all the plans that I have for you, My beautiful Bride, then walk along behind the ones who are following Me. Don't be concerned about impressing others at this point, for you have found great favor in My eyes. But don't try to flaunt this favor I have given you, for it is as you humble yourself and admit your need to learn and grow, that you will receive the instruction that you need. Then, you will be ready to teach the newer ones as they come to Me and even your own offspring," my King reassures me.

"It is not my will that you would know all my plans for your future at this time. Rather, it is through learning to walk humbly with the rest of the flock that your real preparation will come," He continues, "and as you keep listening for My Love Song."

Do not boast against the branches. But if you boast, remember that you do not support the root, but the root supports you.
Romans 11:18

AUTHOR'S NOTE: The Hebrew word for *footstep* is taken from a root word, meaning "a heel, a track, the rear, or the last." The root word that it is taken from can also mean: "to seize by the heel, to circumvent (as if tripping up the heels), to stay, or to supplant." (SC #6119)

I have compared thee, O my love, to a company of horses in Pharaoh's chariots.
Song of Songs 1:9 (KJV)

"You are filled with beauty and grace, My Bride," sings my King, "and you have much strength, though it is the strength of your youthful zeal and enthusiasm — unbroken and untrained. In the past, you have used these to serve other masters. But you are a valuable prize, a treasure to Me, and I am able to see great potential in you, My Bride, as you learn to walk in the ways of My kingdom."

"Who led them through the deep, as a horse in the wilderness, that they might not stumble? As a beast goes down into the valley, and the Spirit of the LORD causes him to rest, so You lead Your people, to make Yourself a glorious name." Isaiah 63:13-14

Why do you gad about so much to change your way? Also you shall be ashamed of Egypt as you were ashamed of Assyria. Jeremiah 2:36

Your cheeks are lovely with ornaments, your neck with chains of gold.
Song of Songs 1:10

"Your words of faith and commitment, your words of love and praise, that you speak to Me are as beautiful jewels, which allow the divine power of My Spirit to begin working in you. Even as you have been led to Me through My Love Song, My Bride, as you continue to listen and respond to My

Song, you will be drawn more and more into My purposes for your life, My love," sings my King.

We will make you ornaments [borders, KJV] of gold with studs of silver.
Song of Songs 1:11

"But, wherever you are, the power of My love and of My Father's love, will surround you and keep drawing you nearer and nearer to Me, My Bride," sings my King.

His other followers sing out in a chorus together, "We will teach you the ways of the Kingdom, for His Law (Torah) is as pure gold. It will keep you on the path so that you will not stray or be lost. His Word gives us light and keeps us from sin."

AUTHOR'S NOTE: *Borders* is the word which is rendered *ornaments* in the NKJ version. According to *Strong's Concordance* it has the meanings of "meander about, especially for trade or reconnoitering: sent to decry, be excellent merchant, search (out), seek." (SC #8447)

We, His redeemed Bride, with His "seal" upon us, are ordained to carry out His purpose of spreading the "Good News" as His merchant, selling (without cost) the "bread" of the Word, the good news that the Messiah came to purchase His Bride and bring her back to His Kingdom through the power of His life given in exchange for hers.

Ho! Everyone who thirsts,
Come to the waters;
And you who have no money,
Come, buy and eat.
Yes, come, buy wine and milk
Without money and without price.
Why do you spend money for what is not bread?
And your wages for what does not satisfy?
Listen diligently unto Me, and eat what is good,
And let your soul delight itself in abundance.
Incline your ear, and come to Me.
Hear, and your soul shall live;
And I will make an everlasting covenant with you —
The sure mercies of David.
Surely you shall call a nation you do not know,
And nations who do not know you shall run to you,
Because of the LORD your God,
And the Holy One of Israel;
For he has glorified you.   Isaiah 55:1-3 and 5

While the king is at his table, my spikenard sends forth its fragrance.
Song of Songs 1:12

As I commune with my King, and my soul is fed from His loving, comforting, reassuring words, I begin to glow with His presence.

✿ ✿ ✿

AUTHOR'S NOTE: The word *spikenard* is taken from a Hebrew word which has a root meaning "to glisten; (i.e. a burner) a lamp or light, a candle." (SC #5373)

You are light for the world.
Mattityahu (Matthew) 5:14 (JNT)

**A bundle of myrrh is my beloved to me,
that lies all night between my breasts.**
Song of Songs 1:13

My lack of background and training begin to fade into unimportance as I gaze upon the beauty of my King. My thoughts are turned instead to the greatness of His love for me. As I reflect upon the agony and suffering He endured because of His desire to redeem me, His straying Bride, my heart is melted within me.

With the strains of His Love Song hidden in my heart, I can rest securely throughout the night. Though I don't possess much knowledge, just

knowing that I am fully loved by Him is enough.
What more could I possibly need?

✿　✿　✿

AUTHOR'S NOTE: *Night* represents a lack of light or
knowledge. In the darkness, the security of His
love means even more.

*My beloved is to me a cluster of henna
blooms in the vineyards of En Gedi.*
                                   Song of Songs 1:14

My heart begins to overflow with songs of love
and praise to my beloved King. "You are a lover
above all lovers, for in Your great love, You gave
Your life for me, even shedding Your precious
blood to obtain me as Your Bride. I had wandered
so far from Your kingdom, and didn't know my
way back. But You came to find me and restore me.
I was poor and wretched, but You have given me
Your riches. I was hungry and thirsty, but Your
Love Song within my heart has been as water is to a
dry parched land. Your love has washed and
refreshed me. It is like coming into an oasis after
long, long wanderings in a barren desert. It is like
receiving a drink of fresh, pure water into my dry,
parched soul. And you encourage me to drink

deeply and linger in this place as long as I desire, drinking, washing, and being renewed. I, somehow, feel the 'blackness' leaving. It is as though I were being washed from the inside out, the 'old' being washed away, and 'brand new' life replacing it. You have given me such abundant new life through Your love, my King," I sing out.

But whoever drinks of the water that I shall give him will never thirst. But the water that I shall give him will become in him a fountain of water springing up into everlasting life.
John 4:14

Now on the last day of the festival, Hoshana Rabbah, Yeshua stood and cried out, "If anyone is thirsty, let him keep coming to me and drinking! Whoever puts his trust in me, as the Scripture says, rivers of living water will flow from his inmost being!" (Now he said this about the Spirit, whom those who trusted in him were to receive later—the Spirit had not yet been given, because Yeshua had not yet been glorified.)
Yochanan (John) 7:37-39 (JNT)

Do not remember the former things, nor consider the things of old. Behold I will do a new thing. Now it shall spring forth; shall you not know it? I will even make a road in the wilderness and rivers in the desert. ... I will give waters in the wilderness and rivers in the desert to give drink to My people, My chosen. This people I have formed for Myself; they shall declare My praise. Isaiah 43:18-21

For I will pour water on him who is thirsty, and floods on the dry ground; I will pour My Spirit on your descendants, and my blessing on your offspring; they will spring up among the grass like willows by the watercourses. One will say, 'I am the LORD'S'; Another will call himself by the name of Jacob; Another will write with his hand, 'The LORD'S,' and name himself by the name of Israel. Isaiah 44:3-5

AUTHOR'S NOTE: *Henna* (NKJ) replaces *camphire* in the KJV. It has the meanings of "redemption price, bribe, ransom." Also "to cover, appease, make an atonement." (SC #3724). *En Gedi* means "fountain of a kid" — our scapegoat — our complete covering — our lifegiving atonement. — Hallelujah!

Behold, you are fair, my love! Behold, you are fair! You have dove's eyes.
Song of Songs 1:15

The King responds to my song of praise and thanksgiving to Him, answering back in melodious praise for His Bride. He sings to me of the beauty that He sees reflected in my eyes as I gaze upon Him. Eyes that once were dark and hopeless, downcast and discouraged, are now filled with the sparkle of new life. Joy and peace, love and acceptance now radiate from my face as I gaze upon Him. The transformation in my heart now glows in my eyes, delighting my King, who exclaims about the pleasure that I bring to Him as I keep my eyes fastened upon Him. He compares me to a dove, also known as a "lovebird" because of the way that it constantly gazes upon its mate. Yet, why would I — how could I — turn my eyes away from such beauty and love?

He sees in me all the perfection that is only in its beginning stages. Yet each stage of my growth is beautiful to Him and brings joyous exclamations of praise from His lips. What joy it brings Him to see His Bride gazing upon Him!

"How beautiful you are My love," He sings, "with your eyes gazing into My eyes, even as a dove!"

But we all, with unveiled face, beholding as in a mirror the glory of the Lord, are being transformed into the same image from glory to glory, just as by the Spirit of the Lord.

2 Corinthians 3:18

The light of the body is the eye: if therefore thine eye be single, thy whole body shall be full of light. Matthew 6:22 (KJV)

Behold you are handsome, my beloved! Yes, pleasant! Also our bed is green.
Song of Songs 1:16

I am moved by His praise for me and sing back my humble refrain of the joy that I feel as I gaze upon Him in all His greatness. I sing out, "Oh, my Beloved, You are the one who is wonderful to look upon. Not only do I enjoy looking upon You, but the life You have given to me in Your presence is filled with such abundance. How could I ever desire another?

"This place where You pasture me has such abundant food and beauty. I have no lack of anything. What a resting place!

"Because of my complete joy and contentment, I can't help telling others of Your greatness and Your love. I desire to bring others so that they might experience this blessing. Therefore, the flock thrives and multiplies constantly. This is a place of 'new birth,' of life restored, of great fullness and blessing!"

*And in that day there shall be a Root of Jesse,
who shall stand as a banner to the people; for
the Gentiles shall seek Him — and His resting
place shall be glorious.*   Isaiah 11:10

AUTHOR'S NOTE: The Hebrew word for *green* means
"verdant: by analogy new; figuratively prosperous; green; flourishing." (SC #7488)

**The beams of our houses are cedar and our
rafters of fir.**   Song of Songs 1:17

"You have provided a strong covering for Your
Bride through Your death on the cross. Your vic-
tory over the Enemy was complete. Therefore, my
dwelling place in You provides complete safety
and protection. Beneath this secure covering I now
am able to experience peace and abundant new
life."

Our house is built upon the *Maoz Tzur*, solid
rock!

*As you come to him, the living stone, rejected
by people but chosen by God and precious to
him, you yourselves, as living stones, are being built into a spiritual house to be cohanim*

40

[priests] set apart for God to offer spiritual sac-
rifices acceptable to him through Yeshua the
Messiah. This is why the Tanakh [Old Testa-
ment] says, "Look! I am laying in Tziyon
[Zion] a stone, a chosen and precious corner-
stone; and whoever rests his trust on it will
certainly not be humiliated." Now to you who
keep trusting, he is precious. But to those who
are not trusting, 'The very stone that the
builders rejected has become the cornerstone';
also he is 'a stone that will make people
stumble, a rock over which they will trip."

1 Kefa [Peter] 2:4-8 (JNT)
(From Isaiah 28:16)

He will be as a sanctuary [holy abode], but a
stone of stumbling and a rock of offense [stum-
bling over]. Isaiah 8:14

AUTHOR'S NOTE: The cedar beams may represent
His death on the cross which provided covering
(atonement) for His Bride.

Questions, Chapter One

1. Who is this anointed one? (verse 3)
2. What does the Bride's darkness (or blackness, KJV) represent? (verse 5)
3. Why does the King instruct His Bride to remain as "turned aside" (veiled or hidden) at the "foot" of the flock? (verse 8)
4. Why does the King describe her as a "company of horses in Pharaoh's chariots?" (verse 9)
5. Why does the Bride describe her chamber or bed as "green?" (verse 16)

Rise up, my love, my fair one, and come away

Chapter Two

I am the rose of Sharon, and the lily of the valleys. Song of Songs 2:1

"I am Your cherished Bride, taken from Your wounded side, given life through Your death (sleep). I am hidden from the power of the Enemy through Your love. My way is made straight, right, pleasant and prosperous, because I am hidden in You. You have filled my heart with such peace and contentment, such gladness and joy. How can I help but sing Your praises!"

AUTHOR'S NOTE: The Hebrew word which is here translated as *rose* is not the Hebrew word commonly used for the flower. Most Hebrew words have a root made up of three letters. This word has several more letters. If the word is divided into two parts, the first part could be taken from a Hebrew word which denotes "hidden" and "cherished" as in the bosom. It can also refer to a "secret" or "mystery." (SC #2244, 2245) The second part of the word may be taken from a

Hebrew word meaning a "rib" or "side chamber." (SC #6763) The word *Sharon* means "to be straight or to cause to make right, pleasant, prosperous." (SC #8289) The word, *shoshannah*, translated "lily" in the text, has the meaning of "to be bright, cheerful, greatly rejoicing." It also means "a white trumpet, from its shape." (SC #7799)

Like a lily among thorns, so is my love among the daughters.   Song of Songs 2:2

"My Bride, I have loved you with an everlasting love — even before you knew Me. I have jealously guarded over you, even before you came to Me, to keep you from other lovers. I wore the crown of thorns on My head because of My love for you, so that My Bride might know My love for her and return to Me."

Yes, I have loved you with an everlasting love; therefore with loving kindness have I drawn you.   Jeremiah 31:3

Therefore, behold, I will hedge up your way with thorns, and wall her in, so that she cannot find her paths.   Hosea 2:6

Like an apple tree among the trees of the woods, so is my beloved among the sons. I sat down in his shade [shadow, KJV] with great delight and his fruit was sweet to my taste. Song of Songs 2:3

"My love, You are precious above all others. No other one was willing to lay down his own life, breathe his last breath, for the sake of His Bride's life and well-being. Therefore, resting beneath the covering of Your love and feeding from Your sweet, lifegiving words have given me everything my heart desires.

"Your words are Spirit and Truth, breathing life into my spirit. They are anointed, for You speak no words on Your own, but only what You hear Your Father speak. They are not just words of regulation, though these words also give me wisdom and protection.

"There is no one to compare to You, my Beloved, for no one else can love me, comfort and feed me as You do. How happy and content I am in Your presence."

AUTHOR'S NOTE: The Hebrew meaning for the word translated *apple* is: from fragrance, taken from "breathing out — even expiring." (SC #8598)

47

Shadow is translated from a Hebrew word meaning "defense or shade, through the idea of hovering over." (SC #6738)

He brought me to the banqueting house [house of wine], and his banner over me was love.   Song of Songs 2:4

As I delighted in Him and His love, He brought me even nearer to Himself, and I became intoxicated by His love — laughing and singing, bubbling over with joy, overcome by His lovingkindness in bringing me to Himself and making me His Bride.

I felt as though I were being lifted into a new realm, a realm that could not be seen by my physical eyes but could only be perceived by my spirit. It seemed as though my ears were also being opened to receive His words — not just in being able to hear them, but in being given greater insight to understand their meaning. And in this realm, there seemed to be an even greater revelation of His power and majesty.

On the contrary, we are communicating a secret wisdom from God which has been hidden until now but which, before history began,

48

*God had decreed would bring us glory. Not
one of this world's leaders has understood it;
because if they had, they would not have ex-
ecuted the Lord from whom this glory flows.
But, as the Tanakh says, "No eye has seen, no
ear has heard and no one's heart has imagined
all the things God has prepared for those who
love him." It is to us, however, that God has revealed these things. How? Through the Spirit.
For the Spirit probes all things, even the
profoundest depths of God. For who knows the
inner workings of a person except the person's
own spirit inside him: So too no one knows the
inner workings of God except God's Spirit.
Now we have not received the spirit of the
world but the Spirit of God, so that we might
understand the things God has so freely given
us. ... Now the natural man does not receive
the things from the Spirit of God — to him
they are nonsense! Moreover, he is unable to
grasp them, because they are evaluated
through the Spirit. But the person who has the
Spirit can evaluate everything, while no one is
in a position to evaluate him.*

1 Corinthians 2:7-15 (JNT)
Isaiah 64:3(4) & 52:15

**Sustain me with cakes of raisins. Refresh
me with apples, for I am lovesick.**

Song of Songs 2:5

The revelation of His power and greatness is almost more than I can bear. Becoming weak and trembling, I cry out to be strengthened and refreshed so that I can remain there in His presence and be drawn even nearer to Him. I don't want the weakness of my flesh to keep me from His presence, to keep me from receiving all that He has for me.

His left hand is under my head, and his right hand embraces me.

Song of Songs 2:6

It pleases Him that even in this state of total weakness I still want to remain in His presence and be brought nearer to Him. He lifts me up, holding me and drawing me even nearer as I have asked.

I feel His left hand supporting me, teaching me and guiding me into His desires for me. Because of the power of His love for me, I only desire to be drawn nearer to Him and to experience all that He plans for me as His Bride.

✿ ✿ ✿

AUTHOR'S NOTE: His left hand could represent the hand of wisdom or guidance. Even in this moment of ecstasy, His Bride is kept or guided by the commandments that He has given to her, yet here in this place of union she finds them not in her head alone but being burned into her heart by the power of His great love.

I will give you a new heart and put a new spirit within you; I will take the heart of stone out of your flesh and give you a heart of flesh. I will put My Spirit within you and cause you to walk in My statutes, and you will keep My judgements and do them. Ezekiel 36:26-27

I charge you, O daughters of Jerusalem, by the gazelles or by the does of the field, Do not stir up nor awaken love until it pleases. Song of Songs 2:7

The King gives the decree that His Bride is to be allowed to remain in this time of "first love" for as long as it pleases her. He commands that nothing is to disturb her in this place. There will be time for her to learn all the ways of her new life later. But for now He enjoys seeing His Bride filled with joy and enthusiasm and "bubbling over" with excitement for all that she has been given by her new found love.

"Don't stop this," He says. "Let this time continue as long as she pleases; as long as she desires to remain here, finds pleasure in this, let her have full freedom here. Let her find her complete

fulfillment in this place until she asks for more —
until she is no longer satisfied and wants more,
more revelation of My plans for her, more sharing
of My life. Let her enjoy her freedom until she
wants more responsibility. Let her just be My
'child-bride.' I love her innocence, her delight in
Me and in her new life, her desire for Me. I love the
joy that I see in her eyes as she looks at Me and all
that I have given her. She doesn't even understand
it, but is in awe and wonderment at being chosen
by My Father for Me. Don't rush her. Don't frighten
her in any way. Don't lay any burden upon her. Let
her be, exactly as she is, for I delight in her! She is
beautiful to Me. I take great pleasure in her. She
pleases Me greatly!

"Don't touch her, daughters of Jerusalem. Don't
bother or disturb this 'new birth.' She belongs to
Me and I am pleased with her."

AUTHOR'S NOTE: The early church had a difficult
time as *Gentiles* came in — Gentiles who knew
nothing, and usually cared less, about laws.
They only knew that being invited into a kingdom, accepted by a King who would receive
them and love them, exactly as they were,
sounded like *good news* — something too good
to miss! In God's wisdom and goodness He did
not allow them to bind laws upon these new
believers, but they were to be allowed to

become part of the congregation exactly as they were with only minimum requirements. The Bridegroom wanted them to get to know Him, to love Him and experience His love — so that He might draw them by His lovingkindness. He knew that without truly getting to know Him, and without fully experiencing His love for them, that laws could not bring them closer to Him. He wanted His Bride to desire to come nearer to Him, to be drawn to Him by His love. He wanted her to be changed from within, to follow after Him and obey Him because of her love for Him. What a loving and patient and wise King we serve! How blessed is He! How blessed is His Bride!

The voice of my beloved! Behold, he comes leaping upon the mountains, skipping upon the hills. Song of Songs 2:8

As I remain resting, content in this blissful love, I am unaware that my Beloved has moved on until I hear His voice calling out to me from above. Searching for Him, I find that His voice is coming from places high above me, places of which I have no understanding, places that from my perspective seem treacherous. Yet, they seem to pose no hardship at all to Him. He seems to be perfectly at ease in these high places, actually enjoying the chal-

53

lenge of every obstacle before Him. So filled is He with grace and power, that the challenges only take Him higher!

My beloved is like a gazelle or a young stag. Behold, He stands behind our wall; He is looking through the windows, gazing [shewing Himself, KJV] through the lattice.   Song of Songs 2:9

He is as graceful as a young stag as He comes to me and stands gazing through the windows. I can see this much — though I cannot see Him fully, for the places that I have opened to Him are small openings, allowing me to *see* only portions of Him and not a complete revelation. But even in this place of only partial light and understanding, I know that I am being watched over and protected. I also know that He has crossed miles and miles of rugged terrain to seek me and find me.

✡   ✡   ✡

AUTHOR'S NOTE: *Wall*, in this verse has the meaning, from its Hebrew origin, "to compact; a wall (as gathering inmates)." (SC #3796) *Lattice* is taken from an unused root probably meaning "to be prickly, i.e. bramble or other thorny weed — nettle." (SC #2762, from 2738)

Though Israel sought other lovers, God hedged up her way with thorns so that she could not overtake them and find them. She therefore decided to return to her first husband - "for then it was better for me than now." Hosea 2:7

Lattice, in *Strong's Exhaustive Concordance* seems to denote that the Bride may be looking through thorns to see Him. Could the hedge about her be the crown of thorns that He wore for her sake? Could this be what holds her, binds her to Him? Love that would not let her go!

Therefore, behold, I will hedge up your way with thorns, and wall her in so that she cannot find her paths. Hosea 2:6

My beloved spoke, and said to me: "Rise up, my love, my fair one, and come away." Song of Songs 2:10

He calls to me, wanting me to come out from behind the walls of *our chamber* — to look up and see that there is so much more that He has to share with me. He wants me to join Him in the heights that I have never experienced, leaving behind the comforts and security of the place of our beginnings, and to come and follow Him. He is calling me to leave my "sleepy" state and to let Him show me new revelations of who He is and of His higher purposes in my life with Him.

For lo, the winter is past, the rain is over and gone. Song of Songs 2:11

He describes to me what life is like outside "my walls." He promises me that I have nothing to fear, for He will still be with me there, protecting me from the floods, comforting me and shielding me in His love.

AUTHOR'S NOTE: The word *winter* here is from an unused Hebrew root meaning "to hide; winter (as the dark season)." (SC #5638) *Rain* is taken from a root meaning "to shower violently; cause to rain." (SC #1653)

The flowers appear on the earth; the time of singing has come, and the voice of the turtledove is heard in our land.
Song of Songs 2:12

"Come with Me, My Bride," He invites. "Let us enjoy all the beauties of the creation and listen to

56

their songs of praise and adoration. We will join them singing praises to Our Father who, in the greatness of His wisdom and love, has brought us together in the wonder of this union."

The fig tree puts forth her green figs, and the vines with the tender grapes give a good smell. Rise up, my love, my fair one, and come away! Song of Songs 2:13

He has so much for me, His Bride, to see and smell and enjoy with Him. He also has many lessons, hidden even in nature, to teach me about His Kingdom and His plans for me. He compares Israel, His Land, to a fig tree putting forth green figs. He also compares Israel to a vine with the fruit just beginning to blossom. He wants me to enjoy the beauty with Him, but He also wants to show me how to work together with Him in His vineyard.

His voice calls to me again, "Rise up, My love, and come away with Me."

"Oh my dove, in the clefts of the rock, in the secret places of the cliff, let me see your countenance, let me hear your voice; for your voice is sweet, and your countenance is lovely." Song of Songs 2:14

"My meek, innocent, devoted Bride," he calls to me, "taken from My side and hidden in the cleft of the rock. Let Me be your strength, your 'Solid Rock' on which you stand, as I lead you into new heights that you have not known before. You have nothing to fear. Put all your trust in Me, answering My call to be brought up higher, so that I may show you new things in My Kingdom and teach you about the plans that I have for you. It is My pleasure, My delight, to share all these things with you as you come and fellowship with Me in higher realms. I will reveal more of Myself to you, more of the mysteries of My plans for My Bride. I desire to have you commune face to face with Me in this new realm, sharing even greater life than we have in our chamber. Let Me share all the secrets of My heart with you. Come, My Bride, come to Me. Lift your voice that I may bring you higher," rings out the voice of my Bridegroom.

... I pray that he will give light to the eyes of your hearts, so that you will understand the hope to which he has called you, what rich glories there are in the inheritance he has promised his people, and how surpassingly great is his power working in us who trust in him. Ephesians 1:18-19 (JNT)

And that it was by a revelation that this secret plan was made known to me ... . In past gen-

*erations it was not made known to mankind as
the Spirit is now revealing it to his emissaries
[apostles] and prophets, that in union with the
Messiah and through the Good News the Gentiles were to be joint heirs, a joint body and
joint sharers with the Jews in what God has
promised.* Ephesians 3:3, and 5-7 (JNT)

*Also I pray that you will be rooted and founded
in love, so that you, with all God's people, will
be given strength to grasp the breadth, length,
height and depth of the Messiah's love, yes, to
know it, even though it is beyond all knowing,
so that you will be filled with all the fullness of
God.* Ephesians 3:17-19 (JNT)

**Catch us the foxes, the little foxes that
spoil the vines, for our vines have tender
grapes.** Song of Songs 2:15

"When My Bride comes to Me and joins Me in the
heights, then I am able to show her dangers that she
cannot see from below," His song continues. "Together we will be able to see all the schemes that the
Enemy has to try to destroy the plans that I have for
My Bride — plans that are only in their beginning
stages, and are even as blossoms on a tender vine
that need to be tenderly guarded over."

✿　✿　✿

AUTHOR'S NOTE: Little foxes usually attack at the roots of young, tender plants. Because of this, the King has much to reveal to His Bride. He has work for her to do in the vineyard, teaching her how to become a watchman, guarding over the tender vines. He knows how craftily the Enemy desires to spoil His planting, but can only suggest to His Bride that she can use her voice to drive the Enemy out of the vineyard. He can only warn her that the Enemy is out to harm the vine and to steal its tender blossoms.

My beloved is mine and I am His. He feeds His flock among the lilies.
Song of Songs 2:16

Though I hear my Beloved's voice calling to me, it is hard for me to leave our beautiful chamber. "I love it here, Lord! It's everything I've always dreamed of and more. There is such joy and fellowship as we walk along with Your other followers. Each day seems to bring new life and fullness. I feel so safe and peaceful and secure here in Your love for me. I'm so glad that You belong to me and that I belong to You," I sing out to Him.

Until the day breaks and the shadows flee away, turn My beloved, and be like a

gazelle or a young stag, upon the moun-
tains of Bether.　　　Song of Songs 2:17

"I want to please You, my Beloved, really I do —
but do You really want me to leave this place that
I've grown to love so much? I know that there's still
much that I don't understand about Your plans for
me and the ways of Your Kingdom, but couldn't
You just teach me here? I feel so uncertain about
what life would be like out there. Could it possibly
be as good as it has been here in this place? Maybe I
haven't really heard You right. Did You really
mean for me to come *right now*? Are You sure that I
am ready to face such heights?

Please be patient with me, my Beloved! Please
stay near and keep me protected. Watch over me
from the heights above. I'll come to You later, but
can't I stay here just a little longer, until I have
grown stronger and have more understanding? I
guess I'm just not ready to leave this place quite
yet!"

AUTHOR'S NOTE: The Bride knows that her Bridegroom King sprang out of (the mountain of)
Judah. She also knows that He came to her and
found her in her *distant place* and extended His
grace to her there. So, she asks that He continue
to watch over her, extending His grace to her
and *leaping over* the great division between

them a while longer. She wants to remain alone with Him in this place of comfort and security, this place of her first love. She isn't ready yet, nor is it clear to her what He desires of her in the higher places. She has no desire to leave and is really not too interested in learning her responsibilities as His Bride at this point. After all, hadn't He commanded that she be allowed to rest in His love and not be disturbed until she was ready!

The Hebrew word, *Bether*, means "separation." The Hebrew word for *turn* means "to revolve, surround or border; to bring, fetch, lead, to be on every side, etc." (SC #5437)

You are fairer than the sons of men; Grace is poured from Your lips; therefore, God has blessed You forever. Gird Your sword upon your thigh, O Mighty One, with Your glory and Your majesty, and in Your majesty ride prosperously because of truth, humility and righteousness. Psalms 45:2
We also have the prophetic word made more sure, which you do well to heed as a light that shines in a dark place, until the day dawns and the morning star rises in your hearts.
2 Peter 1:19

Questions Chapter Two

1. Who is the rose of Sharon in verse one?
2. Why does the Bridegroom compare her to a lily among thorns? (verse 2)
3. What is the significance of the command to the daughters of Jerusalem not to stir up love until it pleases? (verse 7)
4. What is the significance of the Bridegroom "standing behind our wall?" (verse 9)
5. What is meant by "secret places of the cliff (stairs, KJV)?" (verse 14)
6. Why is the Bridegroom concerned about the "little foxes?" (verse 15)
7. How does the bride show her reluctance or her unwillingness to leave her chamber? (verses 16 and 17)
8. What is the significance of "daybreak" and "shadows fleeing?" What is the significance of the name of the mountains, "Bether?" (verse 17)

Chapter Three

By night on my bed I sought the one I love;
I sought Him, but I did not find Him.
                                    Song of Songs 3:1

How could this *place* which had given me such warmth and security, such joy and pleasure, now feel so cold and empty, dark and lifeless? This place is nothing without Him. Even the times of gathering and meeting with the flock don't seem to fill the void inside me. Had I made a terrible mistake in refusing to go with Him when He called me? What was here that was worth anything without Him to share it with me? He was my Warmth. He was my Light. He was my Joy. He was my Security. Not this place! What had I done? How could I have been so foolish when He had called to me as to put Him off? Why hadn't I trusted Him more? Why had I not been willing to leave, even a place that I loved so much, to go with Him? If only I could find Him to tell Him how sorry I am that I failed Him, and that He is all that I really want or need. If only He would call me again! If only He would come to me!

✿   ✿   ✿

Author's Note: Is it that when we grieve the Holy Spirit, by procrastination or disobedience to His call, that He withdraws His presence from us, or by grieving His Spirit do we lose our ability to sense His presence so that we may experience again the emptiness of our life without Him?

"I will rise now," I said, "and go about the city; in the streets and in the squares I will seek the one I love." I sought Him, but I did not find Him. Song of Songs 3:2

My loneliness and misery gave way to desperation. I could stand it no longer. I had to be near Him again, but how? All that I could think to do was return to the place where I had first seen His gentle face and had heard His warm, inviting words. Words that had melted every resistance within me and had filled me with such longing and desire to experience life in His Kingdom the way that He described it. Words that caused me to forget my lowly estate and to yearn to be joined to Him and His followers. Could we begin again? Would I find Him there?

But arriving at the place of our first meeting, it was even as our chamber had become — dark and empty. My heart sank within me. "Oh, my Beloved, I'm so lost and afraid without You, but I don't know where You are or how to come to You. I need You to help me find my way," I cry.

The watchmen who go about the city found me, to whom I said, "Have you seen the one I love?" Song of Songs 3:3

The ones who watched over the flock in His absence heard that I had left the safety of my chamber, and was out in the darkness searching, and came to find me. "Have you seen this One that I love?" I ask. They warned me that it was dangerous for a woman to be out seeking in the darkness all alone and instructed me that I should return to the safety of the chamber.

Scarcely had I passed by them, when I found the one I love. I held Him and would not let Him go, until I had brought Him to the house of my mother and into the chamber of her who conceived me.
Song of Songs 3:4

Seeing the desperation in my heart and that I had been willing to leave my comfort zone behind me to seek Him, He came to me. I clung to Him, desperately. How relieved and thankful I was to have Him beside me again! I would not be so foolish again as to let this most wonderful relationship slip away from me. Since His voice had called me away from the place of our first love, I decided to bring Him with me to the place of my beginnings — into my family's home.

AUTHOR'S NOTE: What is *my mother's house, the chamber (room) of her who conceived me?* Think about this!

I charge you, O daughters of Jerusalem, by the gazelles or by the does of the field, do not stir up nor awaken love until it pleases.   Song of Songs 3:5

Knowing His Bride, that her heart is filled with youthful love for Him, He is willing to be brought into this place with her, at this time, and to remain with her until her love and trust for Him grows. He is willing to wait until she has grown and matured in her relationship with Him and is no longer afraid to follow wherever He leads her.

Who is this coming out of the wilderness like pillars of smoke, perfumed with

myrrh and frankincense, with all the
merchant's fragrant powders?

Song of Songs 3:6

My family was not prepared for the "new me," much less for my Bridegroom King, and I wasn't quite sure how to tell them about all that had happened to me. Would they even believe me if I tried? Would they allow me to remain here with Him if I told them who He really was? Would they be able to see that this One I had joined myself to was worthy of my love and devotion?

But their questions began almost immediately. "Where have you been? You've really changed a lot and where did you get all this wealth? Is it from this one you have brought home with you? He seems different, as though part of a new religion that we have never seen or heard about. Have you become part of it too? He's Jewish isn't He? You haven't gone out and gotten yourself married to a Jew, have you? Oh, well! Now that you're back home again, we'll get you straightened out!"

Behold, it is Solomon's couch — with
sixty valiant men around it, of the valiant
of Israel.   Song of Songs 3:7

"Yes, He is a Jew," I answer them, "but it's not as you think. I haven't really joined the Jewish

69

religion. He hasn't even asked me to, though He, Himself, is a descendent of King David and follows perfectly all that pleases His Father. But He's different, never forcing me nor condemning me, only inviting me to join Him and then giving me the freedom to make my own choice. His love for me is given freely, without demands that I should change. It was His warm, fully accepting love that drew me to Him in the first place. He has many followers, and most of them are from other nations and cultures. His love for them has given them great strength and courage. Some of them have even given their lives as martyrs, rather than deny their devotion to Him."

They all hold swords, being expert in war. Every man has his sword on his thigh because of fear in the night.
                                    Song of Songs 3:8

"These men carried swords, and were trained in using them. They knew that their lives could be in danger because of choosing to join themselves to Him."

Of the wood of Lebanon Solomon the King made himself a palaquin (chariot, KJV).   Song of Songs 3:9

"But He showed them a new way! He knew that His life would be endangered because His Father had told Him His plan in advance, just as it had been spoken of through the prophets. In spite of this, He was determined to follow His Father's will for Him perfectly.

"He accepted everyone who came to Him, Jew and Gentile alike. He never condemned the ones who came to Him, even ones who were brought before Him because of breaking a commandment of the Jews were loved and accepted by Him. He simply told them to 'go and to stop living in their disobedient ways or a worse thing would happen to them.' Because of His loving acceptance many began to follow Him.

"He spoke to them about all the beautiful ways of His Father's Kingdom. The ways that He taught them were above the keeping of rules and regulations because they were not based on outward performance, primarily. He said that we must do all that we do out of devoted hearts, for He knew that it was only through a changed heart that men would ever be able to do the will of His Father. He demonstrated by His own life what His Father had intended from the beginning.

"Because of this, the number of His followers continued to grow. His life and teaching was a great problem and concern to the organized religion of the Jews. Their concern increased as more and more people joined Him and His followers. They were particularly concerned about His claim to be 'One' with the Father. They accused Him of blasphemy and of breaking the commandments and of even leading others to do so as well.

"But He was willing to face their anger and hostility, knowing that walking in total love and obedience to His Father was the only way that others could be set free from a system which had become corrupted. Through placing the emphasis on outwardly performing the commandments of God, it had become a system of rules and regulations, through which many had lost their heart's devotion to the Father. They had begun to trust in their own good works to please Him rather than looking to Him, alone, for their righteousness.

"Though He knew that walking in complete love toward His Father and toward the ones who came to Him would cost Him His life, He was willing to become the sacrifice that would bring the ones He loved so much into *the Rest* that the Father had desired for His people from the beginning."

✿   ✿   ✿

Author's Note: The Hebrew word translated *palaquin* or *couch* or *chariot* has the meaning of a covered litter or couch which had poles by which it was carried upon men's shoulders. In this text it seems as though the King Himself became the chariot or couch. He, Himself, became our means of transportation to the Father, our "Rest."

But we are all like an unclean thing, and all our righteousnesses are like filthy rags.

Isaiah 64:6

Surely He has borne our griefs and carried our sorrows; yet we esteemed Him stricken, smitten by God, and afflicted. But He was wounded for our transgressions, He was bruised for our iniquities; the chastisement for our peace was upon Him, and by His stripes we are healed. All we like sheep have gone astray; we have turned every one, to his own way; and the LORD has laid on Him the iniquity of us all.

Isaiah 53:4-6

He made its pillars of silver, its supports of gold, its seat of purple, its interior paved with love by [for, KJV] the daughters of Jerusalem.

Song of Songs 3:10

"By His willingness to offer Himself for His Bride's disobedient ways, He knew that He could bring His Bride back to His Father, because He knew that this was His Father's divine plan from the beginning. He knew that through His sacrificial love His Bride's heart would be changed and that she would become prepared to be the wife of a King, and be made ready to rule with Him.

"This love burned within Him, the love that He

had for His Bride-to-be. Because of this love, He was willing to do whatever it required to bring her to His Father," I continued.

AUTHOR'S NOTE: The word *pillars* in this verse is taken from a Hebrew word meaning "to stand, or even, to raise up or make to stand." (SC #5982) Silver is the color used to represent redemption. Because the place of redemption was provided for the Bride, she was raised up and caused to be seated or to stand with Him. The foundation or support for the pillar was gold, which is the color used to represent divinity. The plan was a Divine plan, ordained by the Creator. *Paved with love* for the daughters of Jerusalem speaks of the intensity of His love for His Bride. The Hebrew word for *paved* denotes embroidered, also taken from a word meaning "red-hot" stones. (SC #7528) His love for His Bride was so intense that He was willing to give Himself completely to redeem her, or to purchase her again for Himself. He covered her with His grace, garments embroidered with many colors, showing His divine favor.

But God is so rich in mercy and loves us with such intense love that, even when we were dead because of our acts of disobedience, he brought us to life along with the Messiah — it is by grace that you have been delivered. That is, God raised us up with the Messiah Yeshua and seated us with him in heaven, in order to exhibit in the ages to come how infinitely rich is his grace, how great is his kindness toward us who are united with the Messiah Yeshua. For you have been delivered by grace through trusting, and even this is not your accomplishment but God's gift. You were not delivered by your own actions; therefore no one should boast. For we are of God's making, created in union with the Messiah Yeshua for a life of good actions already prepared by God for us to do. Therefore, remember your former state: you Gentiles by birth — called the Uncircumcised by those who, merely because of an operation on their flesh, are called the Circumcised — at that time had no Messiah. You were estranged from the national life of Israel. You were foreigners to the covenants embodying God's promise. You were in this world without hope and without God.

Ephesians 2:4-12 (JNT)

She shall be brought to the King in robes of many colors; the virgins, her companions who follow her, shall be brought to You. With gladness and rejoicing they shall be brought; they shall enter the King's palace.

Psalm 45:14-15

75

Go forth, O daughters of Zion, and see King Solomon with the crown with which his mother crowned him on the day of his espousals, the day of the gladness of his heart. Song of Songs 3:11

"Can you see? Are you able to understand? He really is a King, the Son of David whom the prophets foretold, who came to receive all who would come to Him and take them as His Bride. Because of this, the joy of seeing His Bride be set free from the curse that came from her failure to keep rules and regulations and even from her practice of worshiping the gods of the heathen, He willingly became the sacrifice that atoned for her dark, sinful estate. For her sake He even received the crown that his mother, the nation who gave Him birth, placed upon His head, a crown of thorns."

AUTHOR'S NOTE: Yeshua shared the Passover meal with His disciples the night before He became our "Passover Lamb." It is traditional to sing, *"This is the day that the LORD has made; We will rejoice and be glad in it,"* (Psalm 118:24) at this meal.

I will praise You, for You have answered me and have become my salvation. The stone which the builders rejected has become the chief cornerstone. This was the LORD'S doing; it is marvelous in our eyes. This is the day which the LORD has made; we will rejoice and be glad in it. Save now, I pray, O LORD; O LORD, I pray send now prosperity; blessed is he who comes in the name of the LORD.

Psalm 118:21-26

What if he did this in order to make known the riches of his glory to those who are the objects of his mercy, whom he prepared in advance for glory— that is, to us, whom he called not only from among the Jews but also from among the Gentiles [nations]? As indeed he says in Hosea, "Those who were not my people I will call my people; her who was not loved I will call loved; and in the very place where they were told, 'You are not my people,' there they will be called sons of the living God!"

Romans 9:23-26 (JNT)
(From Hosea 2:25(23) & 2:1(1:10)

77

Questions, Chapter Three

1. Why did the bride finally leave her bed? (verse 1)
2. Where did the bride take her Beloved? What is the significance of "my mother's house, chamber of her that conceived me?" KJV (verse 4)
3. Is there any significance in the placement of the charge "do not stir up nor awaken love until it pleases?" (verse 5)
4. Did the King make a chariot or bed, or did He, Himself, become one? What is the significance of "wood" in this verse? (verse 9)
5. What was the crown that our King was crowned with on the day that He became espoused to His bride? (verse 11)

Chapter Four

Behold, you are fair, my love! Behold you are fair! You have dove's eyes behind your veil. Your hair is like a flock of goats going down from Mount Gilead.

Song of Songs 4:1

"You fill Me with such pleasure, such delight, as I look into your eyes, My love — eyes so filled with love and devotion to Me," sings my King! "The surrender of your Bride's heart to Me, your testimony to your family, revealing the greatness of My love for you, is received by Me, as a sweet offering, even as a freewill offering at My temple."

Author's Note: The Bride's hair could represent submission to her beloved, such as in a Nazarite vow when the hair was never cut. In the New Testament long hair is symbolic of a wife's submission to her husband. (1 Corinthians 11:15) *Gilead* means a testimony. (SC #1567)

Your teeth are like a flock of shorn sheep which have come up from the washing, everyone of which bears twins, and none of them is barren. Song of Songs 4:2

"Your words, your sacrifice of praise, spoken to your family clearly revealed the cleansing, the washing, the *mikveh* (baptism), and the circumcision that has taken place in your heart. They show that you place no confidence in your own ability to walk in My paths, but have placed your faith in Me, alone, and in My ability to lead you, as your Shepherd King. You have fed upon My words from both the Old and the New Covenants, that I have made with the House of Israel, as My Spirit has revealed them to you, My Bride. Therefore, your words will be as seeds sown and great fruitfulness will come from them, My love," sings my King.

Behold, the days are coming says the Lord, when I will make a new covenant with the house of Israel and with the house of Judah. ... But this is the covenant that I will make with the house of Israel after those days, says the LORD: I will put My law in their minds, and write it on their hearts [inward parts]; and I will be their God, and they shall be My people.
Jeremiah 31:31 and 33

*For I will take you from among the nations,
gather you out of all countries, and bring you
into your own land. Then I will sprinkle clean
water on you, and you shall be clean; I will
cleanse you from all your filthiness and from
all your idols. I will give you a new heart and
put a new spirit within you; I will take the
heart of stone out of your flesh and give you a
heart of flesh. I will put My Spirit within you
and cause you to walk in My statutes, and you
will keep My judgments and do them. Then
you shall dwell in the land that I gave to your
fathers; you shall be My people, and I will be
your God.* Ezekiel 36:24-28

AUTHOR'S NOTE: The scriptures above reflect the following words from the text: *washed, shorn* (placing no confidence in the flesh), *bearing twins* — the fruitfulness as a result of allowing the Holy Spirit to reveal Messiah (the one anointed to regather the lost sheep of the House of Israel) to her in both the Old and New Testaments.

*Your lips are like a strand of scarlet, and
your mouth is lovely. Your temples behind
your veil are like a piece of pomegranate.*
Song of Songs 4:3

81

"My Bride, your words expressing the love for Me that you have hidden in your heart, will be even as the scarlet cord of Rahab. It will be used to bring the provision of My salvation to both you and your family. Because the thoughts of your heart are centered upon Me, they are as seed stored up to be sown in testimony as you speak, sharing with others all that is in your heart," His refrain continues.

AUTHOR'S NOTE: A pomegranate is filled with red seed. They, along with bells, were placed on the hem of the priest's robe and represented *testimony*.

> *For Moshe [Moses] writes about the righteousness grounded in the Torah that the person who does these things will attain life through them. Moreover, the righteousness grounded in trusting says: "Do not say in your heart, 'Who will ascend to heaven?' " — that is to bring the Messiah down — or, "Who will descend into Sh'ol?"— that is, to bring the Messiah up from the dead. What, then, does it say? "The word is near you, in your mouth and in your heart" — that is the word about trust which we proclaim, namely, that if you acknowledge publicly with your mouth that Yeshua is Lord and trust in your heart*

that God raised him from the dead, you will be
delivered.　　　　　　　Romans 10:5-9 (JNT)
(From Leviticus 18:5
& Deuteronomy 30:11-14)

Your neck is like the tower of David, built
for an armory, on which hang a thousand
bucklers, all shields of mighty men.
　　　　　　　　　　　Song of Songs 4:4

The words of His song continue and I am completely amazed at what I hear next. "My Bride,
because you are choosing to follow Me and setting
your heart to do My will, because you are keeping
your eyes set upon Me and your ears are listening
for My voice, you will be as a watchtower for Me
filled with weapons of warfare. These powerful
weapons are kept in waiting — displayed, yet hidden in My Bride, not only for your protection, but
kept there for My use until the day that I call you,
My Bride, to join with Me in battle."

Your people shall be volunteers in the day of
Your power.　　　　　　　Psalm 110:3

Not by might nor by power, but by My Spirit,
says the Lord of hosts.　　　Zechariah 4:10

Your two breasts are like two fawns,
twins of a gazelle which feed among the
lilies. Song of Songs 4:5

"How pleased I am with you, My Bride, that you have taken My words into your heart, letting them bring growth into your heart and your understanding. You have received My words of love, that have drawn you nearer and caused you to grow in your desire and trust for Me. You have also received My words of truth, and let them cleanse your thoughts and direct your path. I delight in watching you feed on this pure food, this milk, knowing that you will also be able to feed others."

Mercy and truth have met together, righteous-
ness and peace have kissed each other. Truth
shall spring out of the earth and righteousness
shall look down from heaven. Psalm 85:10

Until the day breaks and the shadows flee
away, I will go my way to the mountain
of myrrh and to the hill of frankincense.
Song of Songs 4:6

My heart is overflowing with His song of love to me, His song so filled with words of praise and encouragement. How does He see such beauty in me, such growth, such strength? I can't understand His great love for me. I feel so imperfect, so immature, so weak — yet He seems to accept me completely, just the way I am. There is still so much that I don't understand but, until I do, I will go to Him. I will join Him in the heights and lift my voice with His, for He is the One who has freely given His life to me, the One who is anointed by His Father to redeem His Bride.

AUTHOR'S NOTE: There is a difference in the Bride's choice, here, which shows that she is growing in her love for her King, demonstrated by her desire to overcome her own doubts and fears and to be joined with Him. In chapter two, when He calls her to share the mountains with Him, she tells Him to wait 'til the day breaks and the shadows flee. Now she is choosing to join herself to Him, even though the day has not *fully dawned* and there are many things still hidden to her. She does not yet feel herself strong or wise, but she is gaining in her ability to see His strength and to entrust herself to Him.

Now in the morning, having risen a long while

before day break, He went out and departed to a deserted place and there He prayed.

Mark 1:35

And being in agony, He prayed more earnestly, and His sweat became like great drops of blood falling down to the ground. When He rose up from prayer and had come to His disciples, He found them sleeping from sorrow. Then He said to them, "Why do you sleep? Rise and pray, lest you enter into temptation."

Luke 22:44-46

Is it that the Bride is learning His secret of *watching* in the darkness until the Holy Spirit breathes His light, revelation, and strength into her for the new day? The word *breaks*, in this passage, is from a root word meaning "to puff, i.e. blow with breath or air, to utter, to kindle (a fire)." (SC #6315)

You are all fair, my love, and there is no spot in you.   Song of Songs 4:7

My King is pleased with the obedience of my heart that is becoming more surrendered to Him. Once again, I hear the words of the song He sings to me, "My Bride, how beautiful and precious you are to Me. There is no guile, no hiddenness, no withholding of yourself from Me. I see the purity of your heart through your desire to please Me. Through focusing upon Me and upon My love for you, your fears have been overcome and you are choosing to join yourself to Me. How beautiful you are to Me, My love! How you please Me in your desire to be at My side!"

Come with me from Lebanon, my spouse, with me from Lebanon. Look from the top of Amana, from the top of Senir and Hermon, from the lion's den, from the mountains of leopards.

Song of Songs 4:8

"Come, My Bride! Come with Me, not in your own strength, but in Mine. Leave the place of your "new birth," your washing, your beginning, and let Me show you new things. There is so much more that I have to teach you, My Bride. Look! See, when you are joined with Me in this height, you are above all the powers of the enemy. Nothing can harm you here, and I will sing to you all the secrets of My heart. My Bride and I will be victorious! Even as I have defeated the enemy, so will My Bride, as she comes to Me in this place."

87

Author's Note: The Hebrew meaning of *Lebanon* is white, washed. *Senir* (or Shenir) is a summit of Lebanon. *Amana* means strong, secure. *Hermon* means abrupt, but is taken from a root word meaning "seclude, or to devote to religious use, especially destruction — to utterly destroy."

Yeshua said, "I AM the way — and the Truth and the Life; no one comes to the Father except through me."   Yochanan (John) 14:6 (JNT)

Therefore leaving the discussion of the elementary principles of Christ, let us go on to perfection [maturity], not laying again the foundation of repentance from dead works and of faith toward God, of doctrines of baptisms, of laying on of hands, of resurrection of the dead, and of eternal judgment ... And we desire that each one of you show the same diligence to the full assurance of hope until the end, that you do not become sluggish, but imitate those who through faith and patience inherit the promises.

Hebrews 6:1-2 & 11-12

You have ravished My heart, My sister, My spouse, you have ravished My heart with one look of your eyes, [with one of

*thine eyes, KJV] with one link of your
necklace.*   Song of Songs 4:9

"You have melted My heart within Me, My sister, My Bride. Your love stirs Me and I have been taken captive by your loving trust. Because you have come to Me and received My love for you and have given Me your love, I am yours eternally. You have opened your heart to Me, and I have brought you into My family as My Bride. Nothing can ever take you away from Me. You are in Me and I am in you. You are Mine forever," rings out the joyous anthem of my King's heart.

AUTHOR'S NOTE: The King refers to her as His *sister* in this verse. Is He possibly referring to more than just their "spiritual" relationship here? The Bride has only seen the King as her Saviour, her Redeemer. It is as though she has looked upon Him with only *one of her eyes.* She has not yet seen Him as conquering King, though she has fully accepted Him for what she is able to see and understand. Because of that *small* amount of faith, even as the faith of a child, He has brought her into His family and put His divine cover over her, the cover of His love. In the King James Version and in the original Hebrew translation, the text reads *with one of your eyes.* It also reads *one chain of your neck.* Could the *one*

eye be referring to "one" House of Israel gazing upon Him with such love and desire that it is deeply moving to Him? Could the "one chain of your neck" be referring to the New Covenant that binds the Bride to her Bridegroom, since she has not embraced Him through the "Old" Covenant or Torah (law)? The word *ravished* is taken from a Hebrew word meaning "to be enclosed; to unheart, i.e. (in a good sense) transport (with love)." (SC #3823)

How fair is your love, my sister, my spouse! How much better than wine is your love, and the scent of your perfumes than all spices. Song of Songs 4:10

"Your love delights Me greatly, My Bride. It is even as new wine to Me, filled with freshness and desire," He sings. "Your love, that has caused you to yield yourself to Me, is the fragrance that I desire. I delight in receiving such offerings."

Your lips, O my spouse, drip as the honeycomb; honey and milk are under your tongue; and the fragrance of your garments is like the fragrance of Lebanon.
Song of Songs 4:11

"The song of love that you sing to Me, is so pleasing to Me, My Bride. Even as you have received My song of love for you and held its purity and sweetness in your mouth, delighting yourself in every word that I have sung to you, even so, I delight in the sweet words of My Bride's song to Me. They are filled with purity and innocence, becoming a pure garment of praise that clothes My Bride. How greatly I enjoy your love song, My Bride!" my King responds.

A garden enclosed is my sister, my spouse, a spring shut up, a fountain sealed. Song of Songs 4:12

"How I delight in the budding fragrance that is growing within you, My Bride. Your heart that is kept for Me alone! You continue waiting for and desiring only Me and watching for My coming. How pleased I am with the dwelling place that is being prepared for Me, to bring Me pleasure and to be used for My purposes! My Bride, I like what I see!"

AUTHOR'S NOTE: In Hebrew, the word *enclosed* is taken from a root meaning "to fasten up, i.e.

with a bar or cord." It also means "to sandal, i.e. furnish with slippers, etc." (SC #5274),

For the Son of God, the Messiah Yeshua, who was proclaimed among you through us ... was not a yes-and-no man; on the contrary, with him it is always "Yes!" For however many promises God has made, they all find their "Yes" in connection with him; that is why it is through him that we say the "Amen" when we give glory to God. Moreover, it is God who sets both us and you in firm union with the Messiah; he has anointed us, put his seal on us, and given us his Spirit in our hearts as a guarantee for the future. 2 Corinthians 1:19-22 (JNT)

Your plants are an orchard of pomegranates with pleasant fruits, fragrant henna with spikenard. Song of Songs 4:13

"My Bride, as one of the congregation that receives its life from Me, your love testifies of Me and is as a light shining forth in a dark place, causing others to be drawn to Me. Though you were an outcast, great fruitfulness is coming through your life, as those about you see your joy and the new life that is springing forth in you."

✡ ✡ ✡

Author's Note: The Hebrew word for *plants* is taken from a root meaning "to send away, for or out (in a great variety of applications), [including]: bring (on the way), cast (away, out), give (up), push away, put (away, forth), reach forth, send (away, forth, out), stretch forth, etc." (SC #7973 and #7971) The Hebrew word for *henna* (NKJ) (*camphire* in KJV) means "a cover, a coating." It also includes the meaning of "a redemption price" from its root word (SC #3722). The Hebrew word for *spikenard* means "an aromatic," and it is taken from a root word meaning "to glisten; a lamp or light." It also has the meaning (from another root word), (SC #5216), of "through the idea of a gleam of a fresh furrow; to till the soil — to break up."

I will make the lame a remnant, and the outcast a strong nation; so the Lord will reign over them in Mount Zion from now on, even forever. Micah 4:7

Joseph is a fruitful bough, a fruitful bough by a well; his branches run over the wall. The archers have bitterly grieved him, shot at him and hated him. But his bow remained in strength and the arms of his hands were made strong by the hands of the Mighty God of Jacob (from there is the shepherd, the Stone of Israel). By the God of your father who will help you and the Almighty who will bless you with

*blessings of heaven above, blessings of the deep
that lies beneath, blessings of the breasts and
the womb. The blessings of my ancestors, up to
the utmost bound of the everlasting hills, they
shall be on the head of Joseph and on the crown
of the head of him who was separate from his
brothers.* Genesis 49:22-26

*Ephraim is a trained heifer that loves to thresh
grain; but I harnessed her fair neck, I will make
Ephraim pull a plow [to ride, KJV]. Judah shall
plow; Jacob shall break his clods.*
Hosea 10:11

(Ephraim was one of the sons of Joseph, who became the head of the Ten Tribes which were
"swallowed up," or "lost.")

**Spikenard and saffron, calamus and cin-
namon, with all trees of frankincense,
myrrh and aloes, with all the chief
spices —** Song of Songs 4:14

"My Bride, because you have chosen to remain in
My presence and have kept your eyes focused
upon Me, your life is becoming a light, a testimony
before your family and others about you. As My
Spirit fills you and you become willing to suffer
humiliation for My sake, it is even as an extension

of my own arm and others are drawn to Me. Because you have let Me stand before you, not only as your King but also your High Priest, My anointing then flows out through you to others and they are able to sense My presence through My Bride."

Behold, how good and how pleasant it is for brethren to dwell together in unity! It is like the precious oil upon the head, running down on the beard, the beard of Aaron, running down on the edge of his garments. It is like the dew of Hermon descending upon the mountains of Zion; for there the LORD commanded the blessing — life forevermore.

Psalm 133:1-3

AUTHOR'S NOTE: See meaning of *spikenard* in previous verse. *Saffron* is a crocus which grows abundantly even in desert areas. (SC #3750) The Hebrew word for *calamus* means "a reed, by resemblance a rod, shaft, tube, stem, the radius (of the arm)." (SC #7070) *Frankincense* — "from its whiteness or perhaps its smoke." (SC #3828) *Myrrh* is from distillation, with root words meaning "to trickle, also to be (causautive, make) bitter, to be grieved." (SC #4753)

(In chapter five, verse fourteen of this book, the King's arms are referred to as *rods*, reflected here in the word-meaning for *calamus*.)

95

A fountain of gardens, a stream of living
waters and streams from Lebanon.
Song of Songs 4:15

"My Bride, as you are allowing My life to flow out through you, others are being drawn. The purity of your life and the joy that they see bubbling up within you, is causing them to thirst. As they come to you, you are leading them into the cleansing, healing, refreshing waters — the 'new life' in My Spirit."

Then shall the lame man leap as an hart, and
the tongue of the dumb shall sing: for in the
wilderness shall waters break out, and streams
in the desert. Isaiah 35:6 (KJV)

Now on the last day of the festival [Feast of
Tabernacles], Hoshana Rabbah [the greatest
day], Yeshua [Jesus] stood and cried out, "If
anyone is thirsty, let him keep coming to me
and drinking! Whoever puts his trust in me, as
the Scripture says, rivers of living water will
flow from his inmost being!" (Now he said this
about the Spirit, whom those who trusted in
him were to receive later — the Spirit had not

yet been given, because Yeshua had not yet been glorified.)

Yochanan (John) 7:37-39 (JNT)

Therefore with joy you will draw water from the wells of salvation. Isaiah 12:3

Awake, O north wind, and come, O south! Blow upon my garden, that its spices may flow out. Let my beloved come to his garden and eat its pleasant fruits.

Song of Songs 4:16

"Oh, Holy Spirit, do whatever it takes to change me into a Bride that fully pleases my King. I need more of Your Spirit to open my eyes, that I may have understanding of all Your ways and all that You desire for me, that I may be strengthened and able to stand against the Evil One, that Your anointing would truly flow out through me, that I might become a dwelling place for Your full pleasure. How I need Your presence, filling all my being, that I may become all that You desire. Let Your will be done in me, Your Bride, even as it is in Heaven."

"Come in, my King, and enjoy all the fruit that You see growing in me. I desire that You find abundant pleasure in me, even as I have in You, my Beloved," is my humble refrain.

✿ ✿ ✿

AUTHOR'S NOTE: The Bride is growing in her desire to please her King. She is overcoming some of her fears, through His love for her. She is recognizing her own lack, both of understanding and strength. She desires to be willing even to suffer for Him, if this is His will for her. She is forsaking some of her self-centeredness and focusing upon her Beloved's desires. She wants to bear sweet fruit for Him no matter what it takes. She, therefore, invites the Holy Spirit to *awaken* her, to open her eyes, to stir her heart, and to prepare her in whatever way necessary to be joined to her Bridegroom.

Awake has to do with her eyes being opened by the power of the Spirit. *North winds* speak of adversity, discomfort — but they produce endurance. Because she knows her weaknesses, she also asks for the comforting *south winds*, as well.

She is asking the Holy Spirit to prepare her to become even as the Apostle Paul, when he said:

I have learned in whatever state I am, to be content: I know how to be abased, and I know how to abound. Everywhere and in all things I have learned both to be full and to be hungry, both to abound and to suffer need. I can do all things through Christ who strengthens me.
Philippians 4:11-13

Questions, Chapter Four

1. What change is seen in the bride in this verse as compared to chapter two and verse seventeen? (verse 6)
2. What changes take place in the bride as a result of her choice? (verse 7-11)
3. How does she become more like her Beloved as a result of her choice? (compare chapter 1:13,14 and chapter 4:13,14)
4. What is the bride's desire for this anointing that now flows out through her? (verse 16)

Chapter Five

I have come to my garden, my sister, my spouse. I have gathered my myrrh with my spice; I have eaten my honeycomb with my honey. I have drunk my wine with my milk. Eat, O friends! Drink, yes, drink deeply, O beloved ones!

Song of Songs 5:1

"Oh, yes, with great delight I accept your invitation, My Bride! How precious to Me is your complete offering of yourself, even being willing to share My suffering. This is the sweetest offering of all, for it is the truest offering of love. How satisfying are your words of love to Me, manifesting the understanding and willingness that is growing within you to become all that I desire. What joy and exultation this brings to My heart, My Bride!

"Come, hungry and thirsty ones! Come and be fed! Eat and drink your fill at this table that My Bride has offered to Me. I desire to share her table with all that would come," sings my King, in joyous response.

✿ ✿ ✿

Author's Note: Because of her willingness to be conformed to her Bridegroom's desires and purposes for her, the Bride is now able to share all that she has received with those that come to her King.

Ho! Everyone who thirsts, come to the waters; and you who have no money, come, buy and eat. Yes, come buy wine and milk without price. Why do you spend money for what is not bread, and your wages for what does not satisfy? Listen diligently to Me and eat what is good, and let your soul delight itself in abundance. Incline your ear, and come to Me. Hear, and your soul shall live; and I will make an everlasting covenant with you— the sure mercies of David. Indeed I have given him as a witness to the people, a leader and commander for the people. Surely you shall call a nation you do not know, and nations who do not know you shall run to you, because of the Lord your God, and the Holy One of Israel; for He has glorified you.   Isaiah 55:1-5

I sleep, but my heart is awake; It is the voice of my beloved! He knocks, saying, "Open for me, my sister, my love, my dove, my perfect one; for my head is

covered with dew, my locks with the
drops of the night.   Song of Songs 5:2

I continue resting in His love for me, but my heart is "tuned in" to listen for the voice of His Spirit within me. I hear His gentle knocking at my heart's door and the sound of His voice calling, "Let yourself be drawn out of this place of rest. Let My Spirit stir within you, moving you to come out of your slumber, to come out of your ease, to take your place beside Me in wrestling against the Evil One who strives to deceive My children and to hold them within his power."

AUTHOR'S NOTE: The Hebrew word for *open* is taken from a root meaning "to open wide, to loosen, plow, break forth, draw (out), let go free, ungird, unstop, etc." (SC #6605)

Finally, grow powerful in union with the Lord, in union with his mighty strength! Use all the armor and weaponry that God provides, so that you will be able to stand against the deceptive tactics of the Adversary. For we are not struggling against human beings, but against the rulers, authorities and cosmic powers governing this darkness, against the spiritual forces of evil in the heavenly realm.
Ephesians 6:10-12 (JNT)

I have taken off my robe; How can I put it on again? I have washed my feet; how can I defile them? Song of Songs 5:3

"But, my Bridegroom, I have already taken off the robes that were so filthy and stained by the sinful ways of my past life. Now that I am wearing the beautiful, white bridal robe, how can I take it off? Or how can I risk having it marred by wearing it outside my chamber? I have walked away from all my "black" past. How can I return to the 'pig-pen' again?" I ask, in mournful tones.

(Or is it the Bridegroom saying, "My Bride, I have finished the work that My Father ordained for Me to do while I was in My 'robe of flesh.' My feet have been cleansed from My time of walking about on the earth. How can I return and walk again among My sinful people? I have already atoned once for their sin. How can I give My life a second time for them? Now you, My Bride, must go out and complete the work of bringing in the 'lost' ones, of gathering the harvest.")

My beloved put his hand by the latch of the door, and my heart yearned for him.
Song of Songs 5:4

My Beloved, then, held His hand, His nail-pierced hand, beside the place in my heart that was not yet opened to Him. As I looked upon that precious hand, that was wounded for my sake, I cried out to be set free from the fear and selfishness that had held me captive all my life. I was given the grace to move out of my slumber, my place of ease and rest, and was made willing to join Him. How could I resist Him? How could I refuse to follow the One who had totally given Himself for me? I could not!

AUTHOR'S NOTE: The Hebrew word for *moved,* (KJV), (*yearned* in the NKJ), is taken from a root word meaning "to make a loud sound, moan, mourn, etc." (SC #1993)

I arose to open for my beloved; and my hands dripped with myrrh, my fingers with liquid myrrh, on the handles of the lock.   Song of Songs 5:5

Moving out of the place that had become so familiar, so comfortable to me, I felt His strength, His anointing, to be able to do all that He was calling me to do. I felt His power within me, enabling me to be willing to suffer for His sake. I was being set free from the things that the Evil One had used to hold me, to keep me from moving out in loving response to the call of my King. Fear and selfishness could no longer hold me captive!

I opened for my beloved, but my beloved had turned away and was gone. My heart went out to him when he spoke. I sought him, but I could not find him; I called him, but he gave me no answer.

Song of Songs 5:6

Though I unlocked my heart's door and opened it wide to my Beloved, He was no longer there. My heart melted with desire as I could still hear His voice calling to me, but I could not find Him. So, I cried out to Him, "Here I am." But He did not answer me.

The watchmen who went about the city found me. They struck me, they wounded me; the keepers of the walls took my veil away from me.   Song of Songs 5:7

The watchmen of "the city" found me and were not pleased with me that I had left "the chamber." When I tried to explain to them that I had done so at my Beloved's call, they didn't believe me. They lashed out at me, angrily warning me that great harm would come to me if I did not return. When I told them that I would listen only to my Beloved's voice, and not the voice of another, they said that I was no longer a part of their flock and removed their covering from me.

AUTHOR'S NOTE: As the Bride, who is now outside her comfortable domain, is wounded, she is exposed (opened up) before others that they may see her. She is "set aside" by her former leaders and left alone. In her suffering, she is made a witness or testimony before others. In this state, of brokenness, the words that she speaks will have a greater effect on the hearers.

> *He calls His own sheep, each one by name, and leads them out. After taking out all that are his own, he goes on ahead of them; and the sheep follow him because they recognize his voice. They will never follow a stranger but will run away from him, because strangers' voices are unfamiliar to them.*
> Yochanan (John) 10:3-5 (JNT)

I charge you, O daughters of Jerusalem, If you find my beloved, that you tell him I am lovesick!   Song of Songs 5:8

Yet, even in my suffering and humiliation, His love filled me. My only answer to the daughters of the city was that if they found my Beloved, first, that they should tell Him that I was lovesick.

The beating or wounding didn't matter. The exposure and being humiliated before the ones who kept the city didn't matter. All that mattered was my desire, my burning desire, to see Him — to be brought close to Him.

AUTHOR'S NOTE: The Bride in this situation, in no way flaunting herself, has lost any feelings of superiority that she may have had. She is broken and humble as she asks for any assistance that they may be able to give her in reaching her Beloved.

But if some of the branches were broken off, and you — a wild olive— were grafted in among them and have become equal sharers in the rich root of the olive tree, then don't boast as if you were better than the branches! However, if you do boast, remember that you are not supporting the root, the root is supporting you. So you will say, "Branches were broken off so that I might be grafted in." True, but so what? They were broken off because of their lack of trust. However, you keep your place only because of your trust. So don't be arrogant; on the contrary, be terrified! For if God did not spare the natural branches, he certainly won't spare you!

Romans 11:17-21 (JNT)

What is your beloved more than another beloved, O fairest among women? What is your beloved more than another beloved, that you so charge us?

Song of Songs 5:9

They seemed moved by what they saw in me and asked, "What is there about Him that causes you to love Him so much? What makes Him so great that you are willing to suffer for Him?"

I was amazed when I heard their questions and realized that my suffering was causing them to be open, giving me an opportunity to share my love for Him with them. They were asking me to tell them of the greatness of my King!

AUTHOR'S NOTE: *Suffering love* is a very powerful testimony. It can break through barriers of resistance that sometimes nothing else can penetrate. It humbles the listener and prepares his heart. It is something that is precious to our King and that He uses to draw others.

In the presence of such suffering love, the on-lookers, "the daughters of Jerusalem," become more open, more vulnerable to the words of the suffering Bride. Her testimony will hold the seal of true genuineness. They also are able to receive her testimony more easily because she is now separated from the "organized church," the instrument which has been used to bring great suffering to them in the past.

My beloved is white and ruddy, chief among ten thousand.   Song of Songs 5:10

"My Beloved is completely holy, completely set apart for the purposes of God, and filled with the *Ruach Ha Kodesh* (Holy Spirit). Through the will of His Father and by the power of the Holy Spirit, He was born as a man, with a body of flesh and blood. Yet, because He lived in complete union with His Father, He was able to completely understand His Father's will and do it. He refused to do anything on His own, but lived only to fulfill His Father's purposes on the earth. Therefore His Father exalted Him and gave Him the nations as His reward."

Though he was in the form of God, he did not regard equality with God something to be

110

possessed by force. On the contrary, he emp-
tied himself, in that he took the form of a slave
by becoming like human beings are. And when
he appeared as a human being, he humbled
himself still more by becoming obedient even
to death — death on a stake as a criminal!
Therefore God raised him to the highest place
and gave him the name above every name; that
in honor of the name given Yeshua, every knee
will bow — in heaven, on earth and under the
earth — and every tongue will acknowledge
that Yeshua the Messiah is Adonai [Jesus
Christ is Lord] — to the glory of God the Fa-
ther.   Philippians 2:6-11 (JNT)

Therefore I will divide Him a portion with the
great, and He shall divide the spoil with the
strong, because He poured out His soul unto
death, and was numbered with the transgres-
sors, and He bore the sin of many, and made
intercession for the transgressors.
                                          Isaiah 53:12

Yet I have set My King on My holy hill of
Zion. I will declare the decree: the LORD has
said to me, "You are My Son — Today I have
begotten You. Ask of me, and I will give You
the nations for Your inheritance, and the ends
of the earth for Your possession."
                                          Psalm 2:6-8

And they sang a new song, saying: "You are worthy to take the scroll, and to open its seals; for You were slain, and have redeemed us to God by Your blood out of every tribe and tongue and people and nation, and have made us kings and priests to our God; and we shall reign on the earth." Then I looked, and I heard the voice of many angels around the throne, the living creatures, and the elders; and the number of them was ten thousand times ten thousand, and thousands of thousands, saying with a loud voice: "Worthy is the Lamb who was slain to receive power and riches and wisdom, and strength and honor and glory and blessing!" And every creature which is in heaven and on the earth and under the earth and such as are in the sea, and all that are in them, I heard saying: "Blessing and honor and glory and power be to Him who sits on the throne, and to the Lamb, forever and ever!"

Revelation 5:9-13

AUTHOR'S NOTE: The Hebrew word for *ruddy* means "rosy" and is taken from a root word meaning "to show blood in the face; ruddy, i.e., a human being." (SC #122 from 119 & 120)

His head is like the finest gold; His locks are wavy and black as a raven.

Song of Songs 5:11

112

"He was anointed with complete power by His Father to be able to do all the work that His Father told Him to do. He could feed the hungry, heal the sick, cast out demons, even raise the dead, yet He used this power only to show His Father's great love for His Bride, His people. Because He completely surrendered Himself to His Father, He was given power to wear the crown of thorns upon His head, and then to offer Himself completely as a sacrifice for our sins."

But He was wounded [literally, pierced through] for our transgressions. He was bruised [crushed] for our iniquities. The chastisement for our peace was upon Him, and by His stripes [blows that cut in] we are healed. Yet it pleased the Lord to bruise Him; He has put Him to grief. When You make His soul an offering for sin, He shall see His seed, He shall prolong His days, and the pleasure of the LORD shall prosper in His hand.

Isaiah 53:5 & 10

AUTHOR'S NOTE: The Hebrew word for *locks* is taken from a root word which can be translated "a thorn." (SC #6977, from #6972, from #6975.)

113

His eyes are like doves by the rivers of
waters, washed with milk, and fitly set.
Song of Songs 5:12

"His eyes were always upon His Father, looking to see what His Father would do or where His Father would go. He could see clearly because He never used them to look upon any distracting or impure thing. He focused them early upon the Scriptures, searching them and meditating upon His Father's words until they completely filled Him and overflowed in His words and deeds. Therefore He became as a solid rock, not moved by anything but His Father's desires."

✿   ✿   ✿

Therefore, Yeshua [Jesus] said this to them:
"Yes indeed! I tell you that the Son cannot do
anything on his own, but only what he sees the
Father doing; whatever the Father does, the
Son does too. For the Father loves the Son and
shows him everything he does; and he will
show him even greater things than these, so
that you will be amazed. Just as the Father
raises the dead and makes them alive, so too the
Son makes alive anyone he wants.
Yochanan (John) 5:19-21 (JNT)

I can of Myself do nothing. As I hear, I judge; and My judgement is righteous, because I do not seek My own will but the will of the Father who sent Me. John 5:30

Sacrifice and offering you did not desire, My ears you have opened; burnt offering and sin offering You did not require. Then I said, "Behold, I come; in the scroll of the Book it is written of me. I delight to do Your will, Oh my God, and Your law is within my heart. I have proclaimed the good news of righteousness in the great congregation. Indeed I do not restrain my lips, O Lord, You Yourself know." Psalm 40:6-9

His cheeks are like a bed of spices, like banks of scented herbs. His lips are lilies, dripping liquid myrrh.
Song of Songs 5:13

"His words are full of grace, fragrant with love and compassion. His love flows out through His words, drawing many to Him.

"His words have an anointing like none other's, bringing joy and gladness to the hearers, for they speak of sacrificial love. His words gave new life to them, as through them they heard of the One whom the prophets had foretold would offer His own life to redeem His people."

AUTHOR'S NOTE: The Hebrew words for *bed of spices* can also be translated "towers of perfume." The word *lilies* has the meaning, in Hebrew, of "brightness or joy."

His hands are rods of gold set with beryl. His body is carved ivory inlaid with sapphires. Song of Songs 5:14

"His strength is given Him from above. It is the power of the Almighty One of Israel working through Him. Through the stripes on His body and the nail prints in His hands, we are allowed to be inscribed there. In this way He became 'a sanctuary' to all His sheep which are scattered throughout the earth. We join with our High Priest, being able to sing out the praises of God throughout the earth, bringing Him glory for all that He suffered for us.

"In His suffering He became our 'hiding place,' our 'temple,' our 'strong tower.' Even as the High Priest who wore the ephod, inscribed with the names of the twelve tribes of Israel, went into the

Holy of Holies with the blood of atonement, our High Priest has our names carved in His body as He offered His own blood for His Bride on the Holy Ark in Heaven. This is the 'pattern' that Moses 'saw' on the mountain, by which the earthly one was made."

And see to it that you make them according to the pattern which was shown you on the mountain. Exodus 25:40

Now this is the main point of the things we are saying: We have such a High Priest, who is seated at the right hand of the throne of the Majesty in the heavens, a minister of the sanctuary and of the true tabernacle which the Lord erected, and not man. For every high priest is appointed to offer both gifts and sacrifices. Therefore it is necessary that this One also have something to offer. For if He were on earth, He would not be a priest, since there are priests who offer the gifts according to the law; who serve the copy and shadow of the heavenly things, as Moses was divinely instructed when he was about to make the tabernacle. For He said, "See that you make all things according to the pattern shown you on the mountain." Hebrews 8:1-5

He shall see the travail of His soul, and be sat-
isfied. By His knowledge My righteous
Servant shall justify many, for He shall bear
their iniquities.   Isaiah 53:11

See, I have inscribed you on the palms of My
hands.   Isaiah 49:16

He will be as a sanctuary [holy abode], but a
stone of stumbling and a rock of offense to both
houses of Israel, as a trap and a snare to the in-
habitants of Jerusalem.   Isaiah 8:14

AUTHOR'S NOTE: The Hebrew word for *rings* (*rods* in
the NKJ) is taken from a root word meaning "to
commit, remove, roll (away, down, together),
etc.," [as in His divine power to remove our
sin]. *Sapphires* is taken from a root word meaning "to score with a mark, as a tally or record,
i.e. (by implication) to inscribe." (SC# 1550,
#1556 and #5608, from #5601)). *Carved* is taken
from a root word meaning "to veil or cover, to
be languid: - faint, overlaid, etc." (SC #5968)

His legs are pillars of marble set on bases
[sockets, KJV] of fine gold. His counte-
nance is like Lebanon, excellent as cedars.
                          Song of Songs 5:15

118

"Because He walked in sinlessness, in the strength of complete purity, He was made the cornerstone, the foundation, the High Priest, the Author and the Finisher of His House.

"His sinlessness resulted from His obedience in doing only what He saw His Father do. Therefore, His vision was not limited, but high above the earth, because He was not led by the flesh, but only by the Holy Spirit of God.

"He became the Shepherd of the House of Israel, which came to gather the sheep which had strayed, and to lay down His life for them so that they could be brought back into the fold. As High Priest of His Father's House, He offered Himself as the atonement for them."

I will raise up for them a Prophet [seer] like you from among their brethren, and will put my words in His mouth, and He shall speak to them all that I command Him. And it shall be that whoever will not hear My words, which He speaks in My name, I will require it of him.
Deuteronomy 18:18

See, I lay a stone in Zion, a tested stone, a precious cornerstone for a sure foundation; the one who trusts will never be dismayed.
Isaiah 28:16 (NIV)

*The stone which the builders rejected has be-
come the chief cornerstone. This was the
LORD's doing; It is marvelous in our eyes.*

Psalm 118:22-23

*Now, therefore, you are no longer strangers
and foreigners, but fellow citizens with the
saints and members of the household of God,
having been built on the foundation of the
apostles and prophets, Jesus Christ, Himself
being the chief cornerstone, in whom the whole
building being joined together, grows into a
holy temple in the Lord, in whom you also are
being built together for a habitation [a spiritual dwelling place, JNT] of God in the Spirit.*

Ephesians 2:19-20

*But you are a chosen people, the King's
cohanim [priests], a holy nation, a people for
God to possess! Why? In order for you to declare the praises of the One who called you out
of darkness into his wonderful light. Once you
were not a people, but now you are God's
people; before, you had not received mercy, but
now you have received mercy.*

1 Kefa (Peter) 2:9-10 (JNT)
(From Hosea 1:6 & 9)

*Yet the number of the children of Israel shall be
as the sand of the sea, which cannot be*

measured nor numbered. And it shall come to pass in the place where it was said to them, "You are not My people," there it shall be said to them, "You are the sons of the living God." Then the children of Judah and the children of Israel shall be gathered together, and appoint for themselves one head; and they shall come up out of the land, for great will be the day of Jezreel. Hosea 1:10

AUTHOR'S NOTE: *Legs* is taken from a Hebrew word with the root meaning "to run after, or over, i.e. overflow." *Pillars* is taken from a Hebrew root meaning "abide, appoint, arise, confirm, dwell, establish, ordain, raise up, stand firm, etc." (SC #7785, from #7783 and #5982, from #5975). *Marble* is taken from a Hebrew word meaning "bleached stuff, i.e. white linen or (by analysis) marble; blue, fine (twined) linen, etc." (SC #8336) *Sockets* is taken from a Hebrew word meaning "(in the sense of strength) a basis (of a building, column, foundation, etc.). It is taken from a root word meaning to rule, sovereign, i.e. controller (human or divine); lord, master, owner." (SC #134, from #113) *Countenance* is taken from a Hebrew word meaning "a view, (the act of seeing); also an appearance (the thing seen), whether (real) a shape (especially, if handsome, comeliness; etc.) or (mental) a vision." (SC #4758)

121

One of the blessings upon the tribe of Joseph, whose descendants became known as "Ephraim" or the House of Israel (northern kingdom), was that he would be *"a fruitful bough by a well, whose branches run over the wall"* (Genesis 49:22). Also, in the blessing over Ephraim it was spoken that *"his seed would become a multitude of nations"* (or fullness of Gentiles, through the Hebrew meaning of the words) (Genesis 48:19). The blessing upon Judah included that *"the scepter shall not depart from Judah, nor a lawgiver from between his feet, until Shiloh comes; and to him shall be the obedience [gathering, KJV] of the people"* (Genesis 49:10).

His mouth is most sweet. Yes, he is altogether lovely. This is my beloved, and this is my friend, O daughters of Jerusalem!
Song of Songs 5:16

"His kisses, through the words that He speaks to me, are as honey in my mouth. What can I say? Everything about Him is beautiful! This is the One that I love, the One who has so greatly loved me," is my answer to the ones who have asked me why He is greater than any other.

The Lord GOD has given Me the tongue of the learned, that I should know how to speak a word in season to him who is weary. He awakens Me morning by morning. He awakens My ear to hear as the learned. The Lord GOD has opened my ear; and I was not rebellious, nor did I turn away. I gave My back to those who struck Me and My cheeks to those who plucked out the beard; I did not hide My face from shame and spitting. For the Lord GOD will help Me; therefore I will not be disgraced; therefore I have set my face like a flint and I know I will not be ashamed.   Isaiah 50:4-6

We ourselves love now because he loved us first.   1 Yochanan (1 John) 4:19 (JNT)

AUTHOR'S NOTE: The Bride's description of her Bridegroom has greatly changed in this instance from the time when she is telling her family "who He is." At that time she saw Him as her Saviour, but now she is able to see Him as Maschiach, (Messiah, Christ) the King anointed to rule over all the earth.

Questions, Chapter Five

1. How does the King speak to His bride in this verse? (verse 2)
2. What does the King show His bride that causes her to leave her sleepy state? (verse 4)
3. Who are the watchmen who wounded the bride and took away her veil? (verse 7)
4. How is this trial used for God's purposes? (verse 9)
5. What is the significance of "white and ruddy?" (verse 10)
6. What is the significance of "His body is carved ivory inlaid with sapphires?" (verse 14)

I am my beloved's and my beloved is mine.

Chapter Six

Where has your beloved gone, O fairest among women? Where has your beloved turned aside, that we may seek Him with you? Song of Songs 6:1

"How are you able to *see* your Beloved, this One who hides Himself? If you *know* Him so well, then where is He? If He has chosen you, to reveal Himself to you, how can we see Him too? How can we hear His love song?" they ask me.

Truly You are God, who hide Yourself, O God of Israel, the Savior! Isaiah 45:15

And He said, "Go and tell this people: Keep on hearing, but do not understand; Keep on seeing, but do not perceive. Make the heart of this people dull, and make their ears heavy, and shut their eyes; lest they see with their eyes, and hear with their ears, and understand with their heart, and return and be healed." Isaiah 6:9-10

*What is more, their minds were made
stonelike; for to this day the same veil remains
over them when they read the Old Covenant; it
has not been unveiled, because only by the
Messiah is the veil taken away. Yes, till today,
whenever Moshe [Moses] is read a veil lies
over their heart. "But," says the Torah,
"whenever someone turns to Adonai the veil is
taken away." Now, "Adonai" in this text
means the Spirit. And where the Spirit of
Adonai is, there is freedom. So all of us, with
faces unveiled, see as in a mirror the glory of
the Lord; and we are being changed into his
very image, from one degree of glory to the
next, by Adonai the Spirit.*

2 Corinthians 3:14-18 (JNT)

AUTHOR'S NOTE: The Hebrew word for *turned* is
taken from a root word meaning "to turn, by
implication, to face, i.e. appear, etc." Also it includes "appear, at (even) tide, behold, dawning,
etc." (SC #6437) The Hebrew word for *aside* is
taken from a root word meaning "to wrap, i.e.
cover, veil, etc." (SC #5844)

In the first chapter of Song of Songs (Solomon)
the Bride asks a question, using similar words
in verse seven. She asks, "For why should I be
as one who veils herself" (NKJ) (as one who is
hidden or one whose face or identity they cannot see) or "For why should I be as one that
'turneth aside' by the flocks of thy compan-

ions?" (KJV) The King answers her that if she does not know (if it has not yet been revealed to her), she should walk with the flock, even following (or walking in the rear) of His companions. Has the King chosen to keep some things hidden, until a certain time that He chooses to reveal them, from both the daughters of Jerusalem and the Bride (or ones who follow after Messiah) as well? Did the Bride really do this? Did she walk at the rear of the flock, as He had instructed her to do? Because of the humility she has displayed, at this time, will her testimony allow Messiah to be revealed to the ones who have not as yet been able to "see" Him? Who are the daughters of Jerusalem? Are they the same as the flock of His companions?

My beloved has gone to his garden, to the beds of spices, to feed his flock in the gardens, and to gather lilies.

Song of Songs 6:2

(The King James Version says, *"to feed in the gardens."*)

"The One that I love dwells in the midst of those who have heard His 'love song' and have received Him into their hearts. His Spirit, His Presence, abides in them and they become a dwelling place for Him. The love that they give Him in response to His love is as a sweet smelling fragrance to Him. He feeds upon it and is delighted by it. As others are drawn to Him, through the fragrance of His Bride's love for Him, He adds them to His flock or congregation of followers."

Or don't you know that your body is a temple for the Ruach HaKodesh [Holy Spirit] who lives inside you, whom you received from God?   1 Corinthians 6:19 (JNT)

For we are the temple of the living God — as God said, "I will house myself in them, ... and I will walk among you. I will be their God, and they will be my people."
2 Corinthians 6:16 (JNT)
(From Leviticus 26:11-12)

Also, when he came, he announced as Good News shalom [peace] to you far off and shalom to those nearby, news that through him we both have access in one Spirit to the Father. So then, you are no longer foreigners and strangers. On the contrary, you are fellow-citizens with God's people and members of God's family. You have built on the foundation of the emissaries [apostles] and the prophets, with the cornerstone being Yeshua the Messiah himself. In union with him the whole building is held together, and it is growing into a holy temple in union with the Lord. Yes, in union with him, you yourselves are being built together into a spiritual dwelling-place for God!

Ephesians 2:17-22 (JNT)

I am my beloved's, and my beloved is mine. He feeds his flock among the lilies.

Song of Songs 6:3

(The King James Version says, *"He feedeth among the lilies."*)

"I belong to my Beloved and He belongs to me, for I am His Bride and we are one. He comes and joins with us as we lift our voices in our thanksgiving and praises to Him and to His Father for the greatness of His love that allowed us to be gathered unto Him as His Bride. 'Hallelujah! Blessing! Glory! Honor! Thanksgiving! Praise to our Mighty King! How marvelous is His Name in all the earth!'" is the song that flows out from the wellsprings of my heart as an ending to the answer of the question that the daughters of Jerusalem have asked me.

✡   ✡   ✡

131

AUTHOR'S NOTE: The Hebrew word for *feedeth* is taken from a root word which contains the meanings of "to rule; by extension to associate with (as a friend); companion, keep company with, ... use as a friend, make friendship with." (SC #7462) The Hebrew word for *lilies* means "a lily (white), also a trumpet and is taken from a root word meaning to be bright, i.e. cheerful: - be glad (greatly), joy, make mirth, rejoice." (SC #7799) Also, *lilies* (SC #7802) means "lily (or trumpet) of assemblage, testimony, witness." (SC #5715 & #5707)

But You are holy, Who inhabit the praises of Israel. Psalm 22:3

Here, I'm standing at the door, knocking. If someone hears my voice and opens the door, I will come in to him and eat with him, and he will eat with me. Revelation 3:20 (JNT)

Yeshua [Jesus] answered him, "If someone loves me, he will keep my word; and my Father will love him, and we will come to him and make our home with him."
Yochanan (John) 14:23 (JNT)

This is the command: that we are to trust in the person and power of His Son Yeshua the Messiah [Jesus Christ] and to keep loving one another, just as He commanded us. Those who obey His commands remain united with him and he with them. Here is how we know that he remains united with us: by the Spirit whom he gave us."

1 Yochanan (1 John) 3:23-24 (JNT)

Oh my love, you are as beautiful as Tirzah, Lovely as Jerusalem, awesome as an army with banners! Song of Songs 6:4

Then I hear the voice of my King as He continues His love song to me, and I am amazed at the words that I hear. They, once again, fill my heart with humility. How can He see in me such beauty and grandeur? Such power? They seem to contain a message, a message that I am not able to comprehend, as though He were desiring to reveal to me even more of what I am to Him as His Bride.

I listen and begin to *see* a picture of His flock as an army, even an army with banners, that is being gathered unto Him. Each of these banners bears His name and is being lifted high throughout the earth, causing the enemy to tremble. It reminds me of the way that He formed the twelve tribes of Israel into an army as they journeyed from Egypt to the promised land, and how fear came upon the nations that looked upon them as they passed through the wilderness carrying their standards.

133

What is He wanting me to see? I can't seem to fully grasp it.

Yet as I take His Words into my heart, basking in His love and knowing that His Words contain the power to create within His Bride everything that His word speaks, a longing rises up within me to become all that His heart desires and His song declares.

"How I enjoy your beauty, My love. I am delighted to dwell in you, My Bride, even as in Jerusalem. As you lift My Name high with your praises, My power and beauty are displayed in the earth," His praise resounds.

AUTHOR'S NOTE: In Hebrew the word *Tirzah* means "delightsomeness." It is taken from a root word meaning "to be pleased with; specifically, to satisfy a debt (be acceptable), set affection, approve, enjoy favour, pardon, reconcile self, etc." (SC #8656, from #7521) The word *banners*, in Hebrew, means "to flaunt, i.e. raise a flag; figurative, to be conspicuous." (SC #1713) The Hebrew word for *comely* (KJV), or *lovely* (NKJ) means "suitable" and is taken from two root words, the first meaning "at home; hence (by implication, of satisfaction), ... also a home, of God (temple) men (residence), flocks (pasture), a habitation." The second means "to rest, to celebrate (with praise); keep at home, prepare an

134

habitation." (SC #5000, from #5116) The meaning of the Hebrew word for *terrible* is "to frighten, or frightful." (SC #366)

Tirzah was the capital city of Israel (the Northern Kingdom) until it was changed to Samaria (Shomeron) by King Omri, who did evil in the eyes of the Lord. (I Kings 16:8 and 23-25) Jerusalem was made the capital city of Judah (the Southern Kingdom) by King David.

Turn your eyes away from me, for they have overcome me. Your hair is like a flock of goats going down from Gilead.
Song of Songs 6:5

(The King James Version omits the word "*away.*")

"Turn your eyes, My Bride, and *see* what I am *seeing.* I am so moved by what I am seeing in you, for I see a Bride who is ready to fully yield herself to Me, a Bride who is devoted to Me and ready to respond to My call, a Bride who is ready to go with Me wherever I lead her, a Bride who is willing to lay down her life with Me. Your surrender and devotion to Me is an offering that pleases Me well," resounds my King's voice.

AUTHOR'S NOTE: The Hebrew word for *turn* means "to revolve, lead, make walk, bring again, carry ... return — turn (self) about." (SC #5437) *Gilead* means "heap of testimony." (SC #1567)

Your teeth are like a flock of sheep which have come up from the washing; every one bears twins, and none among them is barren.   Song of Songs 6:6

"You have received My words to you from both My covenants and let them cleanse your mind and purify your heart. You have meditated upon them and let My Spirit reveal them to you. You have received them into yourself and let them change you. You are becoming a fruitful Bride to Me and My flock is increasing through My word in you and also through your testimony of Me."

So shall My word be that goes forth from My mouth; it shall not return to Me void [empty, without fruit], but it shall accomplish what I please, and it shall prosper in the thing for which I sent it.   Isaiah 55:11

*Like a piece of pomegranate are your
temples behind your veil.*

Song of Songs 6:7

"Even though you are only a part of My whole
scheme of redemption for My people, and I have
kept you as one hidden — waiting for her Beloved,
a testimony has gone out from you. The testimony
of My love for you and your love for Me is as seed
scattered throughout the earth, and through it others are drawn to Me."

AUTHOR'S NOTE: The Bridegroom calls her only a
piece of, or slice of, or even a half of His redeemed ones, reminding her that there were
many who came before her.

*All of these had their merit attested because of
their trusting. Nevertheless, they did not receive what had been promised, because God
had planned something better that would in-
volve us, so that only with us would they be
brought to the goal. So then, since we are surrounded by such a great cloud of witnesses, let
us, too, put aside every impediment — that is,
the sin which easily hampers our forward
movement — and keep running with endurance in the contest set before us, looking away*

*to the Initiator and Completer of that trusting,
Yeshua.*

Messianic Jews (Hebrews) 11:39-40
& 12:1-2 (JNT)

*There are sixty queens and eighty concu-
bines, and virgins without number. My
dove, my perfect [undefiled, KJV] one, is
the only one, the only one of her mother,
the favorite of the one who bore her. The
daughters saw her and called her blessed,
the queens and the concubines, and they
praised her.*   Song of Songs 6:8-9

"Many have followed after Me, even some who
are rulers of nations. Some came to Me to receive
My gifts, but did not yield themselves to Me as My
Bride. Many came and began walking with Me, but
did not continue to let My Spirit draw them after
Me, and turned back.

"Only My dove, the one who keeps her eyes
upon Me, remains fervent in her love for Me and
keeps herself undefiled, is My chosen, My Bride. I
have only one Bride in the earth, one chosen
people, one holy nation, for I AM one.

"You are the one whom prophets foretold, who
at the time of your revelation, would receive hom-
age and praise from queens and kings, even of
heathen nations."

✿ ✿ ✿

*Kings daughters are among Your honorable
women; at Your right hand stands the queen
in gold from Ophir. Listen, O daughter, consider and incline your ear; forget your own
people also, and your father's house; so the
King will greatly desire your beauty; because
He is your Lord, worship Him. And the
daughter of Tyre will be there with a gift; the
rich among the people will seek your favor. ...
Instead of Your fathers shall be Your sons,
whom You shall make princes in all the earth. I
will make Your name to be remembered in all
generations; therefore the people shall praise
You forever and ever.*

Psalm 45:9-12 &16-17

*Behold, I will lift My hand in an oath to the
nations, and set up My standard [banner] for
the peoples; they shall bring your sons in their
arms, and your daughters shall be carried on
their shoulders; Kings shall be your foster fathers, and their queens your nursing mothers;
They shall bow down to you with their faces to
the earth and lick up the dust of your feet.*

Isaiah 49:22-23

*For I will pour water on him who is thirsty,
and floods on the dry ground; I will pour My
Spirit on your descendants, and My blessing
on your offspring; They will spring up among
the grass like willows by the watercourses.*

139

One will say, "I am the LORD'S"; Another
will call himself by the name of Jacob; Another
will write with his hand, "The LORD'S," and
name himself by the name of Israel. ... You are
my witnesses. Is there a God besides Me? In-
deed there is no other Rock; I know not one.
Isaiah 44:3-5 & 8

Author's Note: The meaning of the Hebrew word
for *undefiled* is "complete; usually (morally) pi-
ous; ... coupled together, perfect, upright." (SC
#8535, from #8552) The meaning of the Hebrew
word for *one* is "united, i.e. one, or (as an ordi-
nal) first; alike, ... altogether." (SC #259, from
#258)

Who is she who looks forth as the morn-
ing, fair as the moon, clear as the sun,
awesome as an army with banners?
Song of Songs 6:10

There is a change in His song now as the words
He sings become a question. "Who is she, this one
who has left her chamber and is just being revealed? Who is this one who is reflecting My light
in the darkness and carries My light even where
there is light? Who is this one who is now following
after My standard as I lead her forth? Who is she

who is also lifting Me up as the 'Chief of ten thousands?' " He sings.

What is He wanting me to see?, I wonder. Twice now He has compared me to an army, an army with banners. Is He telling me that there is to be a battle ahead? What is He wanting me to see?

AUTHOR'S NOTE: The Hebrew word for *army* is from a root word meaning "a crowd (especially of soldiers); army, band (of men) company, etc." The root word means "to crowd: assemble (selves by troops), gather selves together, etc." (SC #1416, from #1413)

> *Arise, shine for your light has come and the glory of the Lord is risen upon you. For behold darkness shall cover the earth, and deep darkness the people; but the Lord will arise over you, and His glory will be seen upon you.*
>
> Isaiah 60:1-2

> **I went down to the garden of nuts to see the verdure of the valley, to see whether the vine had budded and the pomegranates had bloomed.** Song of Songs 6:11

I could think of only one place to seek, hoping

that I might begin to *see*, hoping that I might get some insight into the question that He was asking me. I went to *look* into His words that had been recorded by His prophets, the ones He had revealed Himself to from the beginning. Now, I would look to see "whether the vine had budded and the pomegranates had bloomed," as He had asked me to do when I was first brought to Him. Maybe He would now *show* me what He had desired to show me then.

I was really amazed at what I saw, for it was as though I was reading this book for the first time. Words that had previously held no meaning for me seemed now to be leaping out of the pages. My eyes suddenly began seeing that *I* was being spoken about here, not just a "nation" that was only a history of my King's family. For now I saw *myself* as one of the "lost sheep" that my King, who was first a shepherd, had come to restore. Through the marriage covenant that He had made with me, I was now a member of that family and even of that nation!

AUTHOR'S NOTE: "Nuts" are as a storage place for rich food. The shells are sometimes hard to crack, but "richness" is there for ones who bother to crack them. The nut is sometimes lodged deeply within the shell and takes some real effort to remove, but the nut is worth it.

Even so are some of the truths stored in God's Word, nuggets hidden, even as treasures, waiting for those who find the "food" there worth the time and effort of the "cracking," the "digging."

Before I was even aware, my soul had made me as the chariots of my noble people [Amminadib, KJV].

Song of Songs 6:12

I had never felt much interest before in reading about the history of the family of my King. Even the couple of times when I had tried to read it, especially the writings that were prophecies concerning the nation He came out of, I had understood so little of it. All the names seemed foreign to me. The warnings and promises — what did these have to do with me?

But now, as I continued to read and to search into this book of mysterious writings, something began to happen inside me. Not only could I *see* that I was one of the "lost sheep" that my King, who was also a shepherd, had come to restore, but that when I came to my King I had also been joined to a *family*, a nation. I could also *see* all the things that had been prophesied to this nation. Many of these promises had already been fulfilled, but many were yet to happen.

I also *saw* that there had been a breach in the

family and that after this division they had become two nations, the House of Judah and the House of Israel. One of the branches of the family, the House of Israel, had been scattered all over the earth. Their regathering and return to the land, along with Judah's return, was foretold by several of the prophets long before my King's birth. Then I could see that it was through the lowly birth and the sacrificial life of my King that the breach would be healed and that they would be regathered.

The nation had even been referred to as a vine, also a degenerate vine. Had I been part of that degenerate vine? Was I a part of the nation that had "broken away" and gone its own way? Was I one of the "family" that my King had to give His life to regather? Was I a *"prodigal,"* even as in the story of the "prodigal son" that I had heard my Beloved tell? Had I wandered about the earth, even as His Bride, squandering the riches that He had so freely given to me? Was this why He had said, shortly after I had come to Him, that I was as His 'filly among Pharaoh's chariots? Was this what He had wanted to show me when He had called me, at the beginning of our marriage, to "catch us the foxes, the little foxes that spoil the vines, for our vines have tender blossoms"?

All at once, I began to "see." "Little foxes" spoil the root. I had "roots"! I was part of a family, a nation! Then a strong desire began to sweep through me. A desire to be joined again to my King's family. My heart was filled with a desire to help heal the wounds that had come to them partly because of the heaviness of responsibility that was placed on them as "the chosen people." It now became clear to me that "my family," had played a major role in their wounding and that it had resulted from the haughty attitude that we had held toward them. How could I have accused them of being the ones who had placed the crown of thorns upon His head? The "crown" was placed there for my sake, so that He might reach out to me and receive me as His Bride. I was the one who had left, who had wandered about as a harlot seeking other lovers, other gods. Sorrow and humiliation filled my heart. In my brokenness I now longed to serve them, to become a part of their restoration.

Your people shall be volunteers in the day of Your power. Psalm 110:3

Now let me sing to my Well-beloved a song of my Beloved regarding His vineyard: My Well-beloved has a vineyard on a very fruitful hill. He dug it up and cleared out its stones, and planted it with the choicest vine. He built a tower in its midst, and also made a winepress in it; so He expected it to bring forth good grapes, but it brought forth wild grapes.
Isaiah 5:1-2

145

Yet I planted you a noble vine, a seed of highest quality. How then have you turned before Me into the degenerate plant of an alien vine?

Jeremiah 2:21

I am the real vine, and my Father is the gardener. Every branch which is part of me but fails to bear fruit, he cuts off; and every branch that does bear fruit, he prunes, so that it may bear more fruit. Right now, because of the word which I have spoken to you, you are pruned. Stay united with me, as I will with you — for just as the branch can't put forth fruit by itself apart from the vine, so you can't bear fruit apart from me.

Yochanan (John) 15:1-4 (JNT)

And if the root is holy, so are the branches. But if some of the branches were broken off, and you — a wild olive — were grafted in among them and have become equal sharers in the rich root of the olive tree, then don't boast as if you were better than the branches! However, if you do boast, remember that you are not supporting the root, the root is supporting you. ... For if you were cut out of what is by nature a wild olive tree and grafted, contrary to nature, into a cultivated olive tree, how much more will these natural branches be grafted back into their own olive tree! For, brothers, I want you to understand this truth which God formerly

146

concealed but has now revealed, so that you won't imagine you know more than you actually do. It is that stoniness, to a degree, has come upon Israel, until the Gentile world enters in its fullness; and that it is in this way that all Israel will be saved. As the Tanakh [Old Testament] says, "Out of Tziyon [Zion] will come the Redeemer; he will turn away ungodliness from Ya-akov [Jacob] and this will be my covenant with them, ... when I take away their sins."

Romans 11:16-18 & 24-26 (JNT)

Son of man, your brethren, your relatives, your kinsmen, and all the house of Israel in its entirety, are those about whom the inhabitants of Jerusalem have said, "Get far away from the LORD; this land has been given to us as a possession." Therefore say, "Thus says the Lord GOD: 'Although I have cast them far off among the Gentiles and although I have scattered them among the countries, yet I shall be a little sanctuary [holy place] for them in the countries where they have gone.' " Therefore say, "Thus says the Lord GOD: 'I will gather you from the peoples, assemble you from the countries where you have been scattered, and I will give you the land of Israel.' " ... Then I will give them one heart, and I will put a new spirit within them, and take the stony heart out of their flesh, and give them a heart of flesh,

*that they may walk in My statutes and keep
My judgments and do them; and they shall be
My people, and I will be their God.*
                              Ezekiel 11:15-17 & 19-20

*Surely I will take the stick of Joseph, which is
in the hand of Ephraim, and the tribes of Israel,
his companions; and I will join them with it,
with the stick of Judah, and make them one
stick, and they will be one in My hand. ... Then
say to them, "Thus says the Lord God: 'Surely
I will take the children of Israel from among
the nations, wherever they have gone, and I
will gather them from every side and bring
them into their own land; and I will make them
one nation in the land, on the mountains of Israel; and one king shall be king over them all;
they shall no longer be two nations, nor shall
they ever be divided into two kingdoms
again.' "*   Ezekiel 37:19 & 21-22

AUTHOR'S NOTE: In chapter one, verse nine, of this
book, the King refers to her as "my filly among
Pharaoh's chariots" (NKJ) or "a company of
horses in Pharaoh's chariots" (KJV). Now her
soul has caused her to be "as a chariot for her
noble people." The King has commanded that
she not be disturbed and has allowed her to remain "where she was" until something was
awakened inside her. He wanted her to be
moved (turned) by her own desire, from a heart

change. (2:1, 3:5, and 8:4) She is now, of her own accord, "seeing" the vine with its tender blossoms and the little foxes that her King had suggested to her, in chapter two, needed to be caught.

Return, return, O Shulamite; return, return, that we may look upon you! What would [will, KJV] you see in the Shulamite — As it were, the dance of the double camp [Mahanaim]? [the company of two armies?, KJV]

Song of Songs 6:13

Then I hear His loving voice singing out in words that were destined to change the course of my life so drastically, "Return, return, My completed one, return, return! Leave your own people and your 'mother's house' and come with Me to My Father's house, so that We may gaze upon the perfection of your beauty."

What is it that my King is asking of me? Why does He now say "we?" I know that He never does anything apart from His Father's will, so does His Father now feel that I am ready? Is He calling me to stand before Him so that He may look upon me, examine me, to see if I have made myself ready to be united, along with all His *called out ones*, to His Son?

I believe that I now *see* what it is that He desires for me, but what a change! Am I prepared to leave "the house of my mother" to follow Him? I need to be sure that I am really understanding His Words, that I am really *seeing* what He wants me to *see*. I need to be sure that what I have seen in His Word was truly revealed to me by His Spirit.

So, I reach deep down inside me for the courage to ask, "What is Your will, my King? What do You desire to see in Your Bride? Now that my heart has been changed so that I desire to serve Your people and make them my people as well, do You also want me to return to the land? Am I a part of one of the flocks that You will return to rule over when You make us one flock in Your land? Am I a part of the army that will return with You to fight for Jerusalem?"

Now it shall come to pass, when all these things come upon you, the blessing and the curse which I have set before you, and you call them to mind [literally, cause them to return to your heart] among all the nations where the LORD your God drives you, and you return to the LORD your God and obey His voice according to all that I commanded you today, you and your children, with all your heart and with all your soul, that the LORD your God will bring you back from captivity, and have compassion on you, and gather you again from

all the nations where the LORD your God scattered you. If any of you are driven to the farthest parts under heaven, from there the LORD your God will gather you, and from there He will bring you. Then the LORD your God will bring you to the land which your fathers possessed, and you shall possess it. He will prosper you and multiply you more than your fathers. Deuteronomy 30:1-5

For thus says the Lord GOD: "Indeed I Myself will search for My sheep and seek them out. As a shepherd seeks out his flock on the day he is among his scattered sheep, so will I seek out My sheep and deliver them from all the places where they were scattered on a cloudy and dark day. And I will bring them out from the peoples and gather them from the countries, and will bring them to their own land; I will feed them on the mountains of Israel, in the valleys [or by the streams] and in all the inhabited places of the country. Ezekiel 34:11-13

"Set up sign posts, make land marks; Set your heart toward the highway. The way in which you went. Turn back, O virgin of Israel, turn back to these your cities. How long will you gad about, O you backsliding daughter? For the LORD has created a new thing in the earth — a woman shall encompass a man."

Jeremiah 31:21-22

"Up, up! Flee from the land of the north," says the LORD; "for I have spread you abroad like the four winds of heaven," says the LORD. "Up, Zion! Escape you who dwell with the daughter of Babylon."   Zechariah 2:6-7

AUTHOR'S NOTE: Jacob remained in the land of his sojourning until God spoke to him, telling him that it was time for him to return. It was when Jacob, accompanied by his wives and children, began his return toward the land of his father that angels came out to meet him. The place was named "Mahanaim," meaning double camp, for he said, "this is God's camp." (Genesis 32:1-2) Will angels also come out to meet the Bride as she returns?

Questions, Chapter Six

1. What is the response of those who hear the testimony of the "suffering bride?" (verse 1)
2. What is the King's response to His bride's testimony? (verse 4)
3. Who is the only one of her mother? (verse 9)
4. Is the King pronouncing that "the shadows are gone" in His praise for His bride? (verse 10)
5. What change has happened inside the bride of which she is now suddenly aware? (verse 12)
6. What is the King's response to this change in His bride? What is the meaning of "double camp" (Mahanaim)? (verse 13)

RETURN, RETURN
O SHULAMITE

RETURN, RETURN
THAT WE MAY LOOK
UPON YOU

What would you see
in the Shulamite,
as it were,
the dance of machanaim?

Chapter Seven

How beautiful are your feet in sandals, O prince's daughter! The curves [joints, KJV] of your thighs are like jewels, the work of the hands of a skillful workman.

Song of Songs 7:1

"You are so beautiful to Me, My Bride, when you move out in response to My voice. I am so pleased with you when you are willing to take a new step, even before you are able to see where it will lead you, because you are putting your confidence and trust in Me, your King. Your obedient heart is so valuable to Me in being able to bring you into all My plans for you, My Bride. When you put aside your fears and choose to serve Me, rather than seeking your own ease or pleasure, I am able to use you in a much greater way. You are allowing yourself to be formed and molded into the divine purposes for which you were created. I am so pleased with you, My beautiful Bride!"

Blessed is the man whose strength is in You, whose heart is set on pilgrimage. As they pass

through the Valley of Baca [weeping], they make it a spring; the rain also covers it with pools [blessings]. They go from strength to strength; Everyone of them appears before God in Zion.   Psalm 84:5-7

Shake yourself from the dust, arise, and sit down, O Jerusalem. Loose yourself from the bonds of your neck, O captive daughter of Zion!" ... How beautiful upon the mountains are the feet of him who brings good news, who proclaims peace, who brings glad tidings of good things. Who proclaims salvation, who says to Zion, "Your God reigns!"
                           Isaiah 52:2 & 7

And wear on your feet the readiness that comes from the Good News of shalom [peace].
                           Ephesians 6:15 (JNT)

"They shall be Mine," says the LORD of hosts,
"On the day that I make them my jewels.
And I will spare them,
As a man spares his own son who serves him."
                           Malachi 3:17

AUTHOR'S NOTE: This is the first instance in this book, ("Song of Songs") where the Bride is referred to as "prince's daughter." In Genesis 32:27 the angel gave Jacob the name, "Israel," meaning "Prince with God." Jacob was

156

returning to the land when he was given this name. Is the Bride being called the daughter of Israel? Is she being called by this name because she is returning?

Your navel is a rounded goblet which lacks no blended beverage. Your waist [belly, KJV] is a heap of wheat set about with lilies.   Song of Songs 7:2

"Great joy and strength were in you, even from your beginning, when you were still attached to your family. But, now, you have been washed by My words to you, My Bride. My Spirit has filled you and lifted you up, causing you to 'see' and giving you the ability to walk beyond your lowly beginning.

"Now, My Bride, your desire to receive all My words of love to you has produced a garden place, even a congregation, where I am surrounded by the joy and praise of My people," my King's song continues.

Your two breasts are like two fawns, twins of a gazelle.   Song of Songs 7:3

"How I delight in seeing your growth as you

157

increase in your desire to hear Me. You have taken the words of My Love Song to you and hidden them in your heart. As you have meditated upon them, day and night, you are coming to know Me both in Spirit and in truth, in mercy and in might.

"Therefore, your fear and timidity are being overcome and you are growing in your ability to walk in both the intimacy and the strength of My love for you. Seeing your joy as you are receiving My words and choosing to walk in them has also brought great delight to My heart. Through your trust and obedience you are being set free to enter into all the fullness of My love for you, My Bride."

I will give you a new heart and put a new spirit within you; I will take the heart of stone out of your flesh and give you a heart of flesh. I will put My Spirit within you and cause you to walk in My statutes, and you will keep My judgments and do them. Then you shall dwell in the land that I gave to your fathers; you shall be My people and I will be your God.
Ezekiel 36:26-28

I pray that from the treasures of his glory he will empower you with inner strength by his Spirit, so that the Messiah may live in your hearts through your trusting. Also I pray that you will be rooted and founded in love, so that you, with all God's people, will be given strength to grasp the breadth, length, height and depth of the Messiah's [Christ's] love, yes to know it, even though it is beyond all knowing, so that you will be filled with all the fullness of God. Ephesians 3:16-19 (JNT)

Your neck is like an ivory tower, your eyes like the [fishpools, KJV] pools in Hesbon by the gate of Bath Rabbim. Your nose is like the tower of Lebanon which looks toward Damascus. Song of Songs 7:4

"My Bride, you have set yourself to seek My desires and do them, even becoming willing to endure hardship and suffering to serve Me. Therefore, I am opening your eyes so that you may understand My plan for you from the beginning, even what I foretold through My prophets long ago. Even as you were drawn to Me through My love song, you have brought others to come and hear it, as well. Even a great multitude! You have learned to seek after My Spirit, to discern My fragrance, and to follow after Me. Your vision is being lifted above your earthly vision and you are not being led by your natural senses, alone. Therefore, you are becoming a watchman for your people as your vision and understanding of My word and

My plans for My people are being made more clear to you."

AUTHOR'S NOTE: Ivory is formed through endurance and hardship. The Hebrew meaning for *Hesbon* is "contrivance; by implication, intelligence; account, device, reason." It is taken from a root word meaning "interpenetrate ... hence (from the mental effort) to think, regard, compute, ... find out, forecast, etc." (SC #2809) *Bath Rabbim* means "daughter of" — "abundant (in quantity, size, rank, quality) — exceedingly full, plenteous, populous, prince, etc." (SC #1337 and #7227)

Your head crowns you like Mt. Carmel,
and the hair of your head is like purple;
the king is held captive by its tresses.
                              Song of Songs 7:5

"I have crowned you, My love, with the blessing of much fruitfulness. Your willing surrender to My love has resulted in many offspring being born to us. They are Mine as well as yours. Therefore, I am bound to them to perform all that I have covenanted with you, My Bride. Because of My love for you, I will never leave them. They are part of My kingdom, for they are the fruit of My union with My Bride."

✿   ✿   ✿
160

I made your name known to them, and I will continue to make it known; so that the love with which you have loved me may be in them, and I myself may be united with them.

Yochanan (John) 17:26 (JNT)

Joseph is a fruitful bough, a fruitful bough by a well, His branches run over the wall. ... And by the God of your father who will help you, and by the Almighty who will bless you with blessings of heaven above, blessings of the deep that lies beneath, blessings of the breasts and of the womb. The blessings of your father have excelled the blessings of my ancestors, up to the utmost bound of the everlasting hills. They shall be on the head of Joseph, and the crown of the head of him who was separate from his brothers.

Genesis 49:22 & 25-26

AUTHOR'S NOTE: The meaning of the Hebrew word, *Carmel* is "fruitful field, or place." (SC #3760) It also has the meaning of "a planted field (garden, orchard, vineyard)." The Hebrew word for *tresses* is from a root word meaning "to hollow out; a channel or watering box, etc." (SC #7298) The word translated *tresses* in the NKJ is rendered *galleries* in the KJV, with a marginal note saying that the word *held* means "bound."

How fair and how pleasant you are, O love, with your delights.

Song of Songs 7:6

"How beautiful you are, My love and how perfectly you are being conformed to Me! How you please Me! You are filled with pleasure and delights for Me."

... Yeshua [Jesus] answered him, "Let it be this way now, because we should do everything righteousness requires." Then Yochanan [John] let him. As soon as Yeshua had been immersed, he came out of the water. At that moment heaven was opened, he saw the Spirit of God coming down upon him like a dove, and a voice from heaven said, "This is my Son, whom I love; I am well pleased with him."

Mattityahu (Matthew) 3:14-17 (JNT)

Furthermore, we know that God causes everything to work together for the good of those who love God and are called in accordance with his purpose; because those whom he knew in advance, he also determined in advance would be conformed to the pattern of his Son, so that he might be the firstborn among many brothers; and those whom he thus determined in advance, he also called; and those whom he

called, he also caused to be considered righ-
teous; and those whom he caused to be
considered righteous, he also glorified!

Romans 8:28-30 (JNT)

AUTHOR'S NOTE: The Hebrew word for *pleasant* is
taken from a root word meaning "to be agree-
able." (SC #5276)

This stature of yours is like a palm tree,
and your breasts like its clusters [of
grapes, KJV].   Song of Songs 7:7

"You walk uprightly before Me, My Bride. As
you have risen up in obedience to 'My call' to you,
you are finding greater strength to endure. Your
vision is becoming more clear so that you may be
able to see and to walk in the 'higher calling' of My
Bride.

"As your roots have gone down deeper, and you
have again seen your family in the storehouse of
My words, it has given you clearer vision of My
plans for your future. As My Bride responds, she is
being drawn together, even with others who are
being awakened and who are responding to My
call to My Bride, and a tender new cluster of fruit is
beginning to be formed on the vine," rejoices my
King over me in love.

✿   ✿   ✿

AUTHOR'S NOTE: *Stature* is taken from a Hebrew word meaning "height." The root word that it is derived from has a variety of meanings including "to rise, be clearer, enjoin, get up, pitch, raise up, establish, make to stand up, etc." (SC #6967, from #6965) *Cluster* is from a Hebrew word meaning "to bunch together." (SC #811) *Grapes* is from a Hebrew word meaning "a vine blossom." (SC #5563)

The root of a palm tree goes straight down and very deep, allowing for its straight, tall nature. This also gives it its ability to withstand high winds and storms.

I said, "I will go up to the palm tree, I will take hold of its branches [boughs, KJV]. Let now your breasts be like clusters of the vine, the fragrance of your breath like apples." Song of Songs 7:8

"I will do now, even as I have spoken to you before. I will come to you and possess you, even for My own. I will drink and be lifted up with the wine of your love and by your willingness, My Bride, to fully yield yourself to My Spirit that dwells within you."

The way of the just is uprightness; O Most Upright, You weigh the path of the just. ... O Lord, we have waited for You; the desire of our soul is for Your name and for the remembrance of You. With my soul I have desired You in the night, Yes, by my spirit within me I will seek You early; for when Your judgments are in the earth, the inhabitants of the world will learn righteousness. ... LORD, You will establish peace for us, for You have also done all our works in us.   Isaiah 26:7-9 & 12

AUTHOR'S NOTE: The Hebrew word for *boughs* means "to be pointed; a twig (as tapering), a bough." The Hebrew word for *smell* is taken from a root word meaning "to blow i.e. breathe: only (literally) to smell or, by implication, perceive, make of quick understanding." It is the same as the word used for spirit, as in Holy Spirit. (SC #7381, from #7306)

I will sow them among the peoples, and they shall remember Me in far countries; They shall live together with their children, and they shall return. ... And I will save the house of Joseph. I will bring them back because I have mercy on them. They shall be as though I had not cast them aside; for I am the LORD their God, and I will hear them. Those of Ephraim shall be like a mighty man, and their heart shall rejoice as if with wine.   Zechariah 10:9 & 6-7

As the Father ran out to meet the prodigal son when he was "yet a long way off," *even so the Bridegroom joins Himself to His Bride as she begins her* "return."

Again, the prophecy spoken over Joseph, Genesis, chapter 49, says that *"Joseph is a fruitful bough, a fruitful bough by a well."* It also says that his branches (offspring) run over the wall. The archers have bitterly grieved him, shot at him and hated him. All the blessings that were promised were spoken of as *"on the crown of the head of him who was separate from his brothers"* (Genesis 49:22-26).

And the roof of your mouth like the best wine. The wine goes down smoothly for my beloved, moving gently the lips of sleepers.   Song of Songs 7:9

"Your words, My Bride, the kisses of your mouth, are the sweetest wine to Me. For, your response is 'Yes,' to my request to you.

"It is as though you have drunk deeply of the words that My prophets spoke long ago, foretelling My Bride's return. Your words are in agreement, My Bride, and are causing the words of the prophets to be fulfilled in you."

✿ ✿ ✿

Therefore prophesy and say to them, "Thus says the Lord GOD; 'Behold, O My people, I will open your graves and cause you to come up from your graves, and bring you into the land of Israel. Then you shall know that I am the LORD, when I have opened your graves, O My people, and brought you up from your graves. I will put My Spirit in you, and you shall live, and I will place you in your own land. Then you shall know that I, the LORD, have spoken it and performed it, says the LORD.' "   Ezekiel 37:12-14

Your dead shall live; together with my dead body they shall arise. Awake and sing, you who dwell in the dust; for your dew is like the dew of herbs, and the earth shall cast out the dead.   Isaiah 26:19

Get up, sleeper! Arise from the dead, and the Messiah will shine on you!
                                        Ephesians 5:14 (JNT)

AUTHOR'S NOTE: Though the Bridegroom commanded that His Bride not be disturbed, (Song of Songs 2:17, 3:5, 8:4), but that she could remain as she was (sleeping) "until it pleased" her to arise, He is delighted with her response at His call to her to "arise" and "return."

167

***I am my beloved's, and His desire is to-
ward me.*** Song of Songs 7:10

"I belong to You, my King. I shall be forever grateful that You desire me as Your Bride. As I have come to know You better, I can see that You have loved me from the beginning and planned for me even before I was born. Your great plan for Your Bride has always been for my good, to bless Your Bride and to bring her nearer to You. How blessed I am to be Your Bride!"

✿ ✿ ✿

Thus says the LORD: "The people who survived the sword found grace in the wilderness — Israel, when I went to give him rest." The LORD has appeared of old to me saying: "Yes, I have loved you with an everlasting love; therefore with lovingkindness I have drawn you. Again, I will build you and you shall be rebuilt, O virgin of Israel! You shall again be adorned with your tambourines, and shall go forth in the dances of those who rejoice. You shall yet plant vines on the mountains of Samaria; ... For there shall be a day when the watchmen will cry on Mount Ephraim, 'Arise, and let us go up to Zion, to the LORD our God.' Jeremiah 31:2-6

Hear the word of the LORD, O nations [Gentiles], and declare it in the isles [coastlines] afar off, and say, 'He who scattered Israel will gather him, and keep him as a shepherd does his flock.' For the Lord has redeemed Jacob, and ransomed him from the hand of one stronger than he. Therefore they shall come and sing in the height of Zion, streaming to the goodness of the LORD — for wheat and new wine and oil, for the young of the flock and the herd; their souls shall be like a well-watered garden, and they shall sorrow no more at all.

Jeremiah 31:10-12

For the LORD has redeemed Jacob, and ransomed him from the hand of one stronger than he.' ... 'Refrain your voice from weeping, and your eyes from tears; for your work shall be rewarded,' says the LORD, 'and they shall come back from the land of the enemy. There is hope in your future, says the LORD, that your children shall come back to their own border. ... And it shall come to pass, that as I have watched over them to pluck up, to break down, to throw down, to destroy, and to afflict, so I will watch over them to build and to plant,' says the LORD. Jeremiah 31:16-17 & 28

'Behold the days are coming,' says the LORD, when I will make a new covenant with the house of Israel and with the house of Judah —

not according to the covenant that I made with their fathers in the day that I took them by the hand to bring them out of the land of Egypt, My covenant which they broke, though I was a husband to them, says the LORD. But this is the covenant that I will make with the house of Israel after those days, says the LORD: I will put My law in their minds, and write it on their hearts; and I will be their God, and they shall be my people. Jeremiah 31:31-33

Come, my beloved, let us go forth, to the field; let us lodge in the villages.
Song of Songs 7:11

"Because I know that You are with me, my beloved Bridegroom, I am ready to leave this place where You found me. I am ready to make the journey with You. Your desire is now my desire. Let us return!"

Sing to the LORD a new song, and His praise from the ends of the earth, you who go down to the sea and all that is in it, you coastlands and you inhabitants of them! Let the wilderness and its cities lift up their voice, the villages that Kedar inhabits. Let the inhabitants of Sela sing, let them shout from the top of the

mountains. Let them give glory to the LORD, and declare His praise in the coastlands. The LORD shall go forth like a mighty man; he shall stir up His zeal like a man of war. He shall cry out, yes, shout aloud; he shall prevail against his enemies.   Isaiah 42:10-13

Is Ephraim My dear son? Is he a pleasant child? For though I spoke against him, I earnestly remember him still; therefore My heart yearns for him; I will surely have mercy on him, says the LORD. Set up signposts, make landmarks; set your heart toward the highway, the way in which you went. Turn back [return] O virgin of Israel, turn back to these your cities. How long will you gad about, O you backsliding daughter? For the LORD has created a new thing in the earth — A woman shall encompass a man.   Jeremiah 31:20-22

Let us get up early to the vineyards; let us see if the vine has budded [flourish, KJV], whether the [tender, KJV] grape blossoms are open [appear, KJV] and the pomegranates are in bloom. There I will give you my love.   Song of Songs 7:12

"Now that my eyes have been opened and I have seen that as Your Bride I have been made a part of

171

the vine, I want to rise up early to care for it. Even as You have so desired that Your vineyard be watched over, let us watch together. Let us walk among "our people" and see where eyes are beginning to be opened to You, to see the ones that may be ready to receive Your love. Here I will freely give You my love, my Bridegroom."

What follows is that Israel has not attained the goal for which she is striving. The ones chosen have obtained it, but the rest have been made stonelike, just as the Tanakh (Old Testament) says, 'God has given them a spirit of dullness — eyes that do not see and ears that do not hear right down to the present day.' And David says, 'Let their dining table become for them a snare and a trap, a pitfall and a punishment. Let their eyes be darkened, so that they can't see, with their backs bent continually.' In that case, I say, isn't it that they have stumbled with the result that they have permanently fallen away? Heaven forbid! Quite the contrary, it is by means of their stumbling that the deliverance has come to the Gentiles, in order to provoke them to jealousy.

Romans 11:7-11 (JNT)
(From Deuteronomy 29:4,
Isaiah 29:10 & Psalm 69:22-23)

172

The mandrakes give off a fragrance, and at our gates are pleasant fruits, all manner, new and old, which I have laid up for you, my beloved. Song of Songs 7:13

"You were anointed by Your Father, my King, to draw Your Bride to Yourself; but now the fragrance of Your Bride's love and her strong desire to fully yield herself to You and become one with You, is causing You to be drawn to her as well. This place of more complete union with You has brought us to a gateway of riches. It is as though You have opened a storehouse of wealth, my Beloved, as Your words have revealed to me both my past and even now are beginning to show me the future that I have with You as Your Bride.

"Oh, the riches of Your love, my King! Your treasure has been hidden in Your Bride, both in ages past and in this present age. All of it has been kept for You, my Beloved!"

Oh, how great is Your goodness, which You have laid up for those who fear You which You have prepared for those who trust in you in the presence of the sons of men. You shall hide them in the secret place of Your presence. ...

Blessed be the LORD, for He has shown me
His marvelous kindness in a strong city.

Psalm 31:19-21

Who is the man that fears the LORD? Him
shall He teach in the way He chooses. He
himself shall dwell in prosperity, and his de-
scendants shall inherit the earth. The secret of
the LORD is with those who fear Him, and He
will show them His covenant.

Psalm 25:12-14

On the contrary, we are communicating a se-
cret wisdom from God which has been hidden
until now but which, before history began,
God had decreed would bring us glory. Not
one of this world's leaders has understood it;
because if they had, they would not have ex-
ecuted the Lord from whom this glory flows.
But, as the Tanakh [Old Testament] says, 'No
eye has seen, no ear has heard and no one's
heart has imagined all the things God has pre-
pared for those who love him.' It is to us,
however, that God has revealed these things.
How? Through the Spirit. For the Spirit
probes all things, even the profoundest depths
of God. For who knows the inner workings of a
person except the person's own spirit inside
him? So too no one knows the inner workings
of God except God's Spirit. Now we have not
received the spirit of the world but the Spirit of

God, so that we might understand the things
God has so freely given us.
1 Corinthians 2:7-12 (JNT)

AUTHOR'S NOTE: The Hebrew word for *mandrakes* is "a boiler, or a basket." (SC #1736) The Hebrew word for *gates* means "opening, door," and is taken from a root word meaning "to open wide, loosen, appear, break forth, etc." (SC #6607 from #6605) The Hebrew word for *laid* means "to hide (by covering over); reserve, protect, (keep) secret (-ly place)." (SC #6845)

Questions, Chapter Seven

1. Why does the King now refer to His bride as "prince's daughter?" (verse 1)
2. What is the significance of the words the King used to describe His bride's eyes, "Hesbon" — by the gate of "Bath Rabbim?" (verse 4)
3. Who are the "sleepers?" (verse 9)
4. Why is the bride now inviting the King to get up early and examine the new blossoms on the vine? (verse 12)
5. What do you think has brought about the change in the bride since her refusal to join the King in His invitation to her in chapter two, verses ten through thirteen? (verse 12)

Chapter Eight

Oh that you were like my brother, Who nursed at my mother's breasts! If I should find you outside, I would kiss you; I would not be despised.

Song of Songs 8:1

"I'm afraid, my Beloved, that when I return with You to Your family that they won't receive me. It would be much more comfortable for me if you were more like 'my family,' like the Gentile nations who nurtured me. If you were more like them, I could speak of my love for You more openly and not feel their hatred and rejection."

I would lead you and bring you into the house of my mother, she who used to instruct me. I would cause you to drink of spiced wine, of the juice of my pomegranate.　Song of Songs 8:2

"I love You, but this is really stretching me! It would be much more comfortable for me to take You into the congregations of my family, as we pass through the lands. Since I received my child-hood training from them, my testimony would be much more acceptable to them. I could share the testimony of my love for You openly there and they will love You too. We could share fellowship and communion with them."

His left hand is under my head, and his right hand embraces me.

Song of Songs 8:3

"He is my covering, so that I need not trust in my own ability to walk by His Word, for there are yet many things that my mind cannot comprehend. It is only in His nail pierced hands, drawing me to Himself, enfolding me in His love, and guiding me each step of the way, that I trust," I say to encourage myself as I see the ones who are staring at me as we walk up to the gate.

Therefore, there is no longer any condemnation awaiting those who are in union with the Messiah Yeshua [Christ Jesus]. Why? Because the Torah [law] of the Spirit, which produces this life in union with Messiah Yeshua, has set me free from the "torah" of sin and death. ... Having one's mind controlled by the old na-

178

ture is death, but having one's mind controlled by the Spirit is life and shalom [peace]. For the mind controlled by the old nature is hostile to God, because it does not submit itself to God's Torah — indeed, it cannot. Thus, those who identify with their old nature cannot please God. But you, you do not identify with your old nature but with the Spirit — provided the Spirit of God is living inside you, for anyone who doesn't have the Spirit of the Messiah doesn't belong to Him. ... All who are led by God's Spirit are God's sons. For you did not receive a spirit of slavery to bring you back again into fear; on the contrary, you received the Spirit, who makes us sons, and by whose power we cry out, "Abba!" (that is, "Dear Father!") The Spirit himself bears witness with our own spirits that we are children of God; and if we are children, then we are also heirs, heirs of God and joint-heirs with the Messiah — provided we are suffering with him in order also to be glorified with him.

Romans 8:1-2, 6-9 & 14-17 (JNT)

AUTHOR'S NOTE: The Hebrew word for *left* is taken from another Hebrew word meaning "wrapping up, (as enveloped) i.e. the north; also, the idea of a cover assuming the shape of the object beneath; especially, a mantle, etc." (SC #8040, from #8071) The Hebrew word for *hand* means "a hand (the open one [indicating power,

179

means, direction] in distinction from #3709, the closed one)." The meaning of the Hebrew word for #3709 is "the hollow hand or palm, the handle of a bolt." This is the hand that was placed by the bolt of the Bride's door in chapter five, verse four.

I charge you, O daughters of Jerusalem, do not stir up nor awaken love until it pleases. Song of Songs 8:4

"It has been commanded, daughters of Jerusalem, My Son's Bride, that you be fully ready to completely yield yourselves, to pour yourselves out in your love for your Bridegroom, when you come to the wedding feast. You must be ready to leave your family and everything of your past behind you, if you would be joined to My Son. His Bride must see and desire only Him. She must be consumed by her love for Him alone. Only then will she be prepared to be fully joined to My Son," speaks a voice from above.

Listen, O daughter, consider and incline your ear; forget your own people also, and your father's house; So the King will greatly desire

your beauty; because He is your Lord, worship Him.   Psalm 45:10-11

Yes, I gave it all up in order to know him, that is, to know the power of his resurrection and the fellowship of his sufferings as I am being conformed to his death, so that somehow I might arrive at being resurrected from the dead. It is not that I have already obtained it or already reached the goal — no, I keep pursuing it in the hope of taking hold of that for which the Messiah Yeshua took hold of me.   Philippians 3:10-12 (JNT)

Let us rejoice and be glad! Let us give him the glory! For the time has come for the wedding of the Lamb, and His Bride has prepared herself.   Revelation 19:7 (JNT)

Who is this coming up from the wilderness, leaning upon her beloved? I awakened you under the apple tree. There your mother brought you forth. There she who bore you, brought you forth.   Song of Songs 8:5

As we come nearer to the ones who are dwelling in the land, I can hear them as they talk among themselves saying, "Who is this one who is coming

181

from the heathen nations, and claiming that she is now part of the family, and part of the nation, as the Bride of Messiah?"

"Weren't we told that we were the ones who were awakened to His love? Weren't we the ones brought forth by Him, the ones He called His children, and even His Bride? Is this one now coming, calling herself Messiah's Bride, going to try to take away our inheritance and claim our Beloved as her own?" they continue.

Then I hear my Bridegroom's voice comforting me, saying, "You were also part of the nation that I called to Myself long ago, My daughter. Even before your mother bore you, I knew you and called you by your name. Have no fear!"

For the LORD'S portion is His people; Jacob is the place of His inheritance. He found him in a desert land and in the wasteland, a howling wilderness; He encircled [encompassed] him, He instructed him, He kept him as the apple of His eye. Deuteronomy 32:9-10

Praised be Adonai [the LORD], Father of our Lord Yeshua the Messiah, who in the Messiah has blessed us with every spiritual blessing in heaven. In the Messiah he chose us in love before the creation of the universe to be holy and without defect in his presence. He determined in advance that through Yeshua the Messiah we would be his sons — in keeping with his pleasure and purpose — so that we would bring him the praise commensurate with the glory of the grace he gave us through the Beloved One.   Ephesians 1:3-6 (JNT)

Set me as a seal upon your heart, as a seal upon your arm; for love is as strong as death, jealousy as cruel as the grave; Its flames are flames of fire, a most vehement flame.   Song of Songs 8:6

"Keep your mind and heart stayed on Me, My Bride. Let your love for Me, and My love for you, become your strength. Their jealousy may be strong and you may even have to suffer for calling yourself by My name, but by keeping your heart set upon loving Me and upon loving your family, all fear will be cast out. Love will give you courage and strength to overcome every power that can come against you, the power of jealousy and the power of the grave. Even death and hell will be overcome by the power of My love for you and your love for Me, My Bride," His song encourages me.

✡ ✡ ✡

This is his command: that we are to trust in the person and power of his Son Yeshua the Messiah and to keep loving one another, just as he commanded us. Those who obey his commands remain united with him and he with them. ... Beloved friends, let us love one another; because love is from God; and everyone who loves has God as his Father and knows God. Those who do not love, do not know God; because God is love. Here is how God showed his love among us: God sent his only Son into the world, so that through him we might have life. Here is what love is: not that we have loved God, but that he loved us and sent his Son to be the kapparah [atonement] for our sins. Beloved friends, if this is how God loved us, we likewise ought to love one another. No one has ever seen God; if we love one another, God remains united with us, and our love for him has been brought to its goal in us. Here is how that we remain united with him and he with us: he has given to us from his own Spirit. Moreover, we have seen and we testify that the Father has sent his Son as Deliverer of the world. If someone acknowledges that Yeshua [Jesus] is the Son of God, God remains united with him, and he with God. Also we have come to know and trust the love that God has for us. God is love; and those who remain in this love remain united with God, and God remains united with them. Here is how love has been brought to maturity with us: as the Messiah is, so are we in the world. This gives us confidence for the Day of Judgement. There is no fear in love. On the contrary, love that has achieved its goal gets rid of fear, because fear has to do with punishment; the person who keeps fearing has not been brought to maturity in regard to love. We ourselves love now because he loved us first. If anyone says, 'I love God,' and hates his brother, he is a liar. For if a person does not love his brother, whom he has seen, then he cannot love God, whom he has not seen. Yes, this is the command we have from him: whoever loves God must love his brother too.

1 Yochanan (1 John) 3:23-24 & 4:7-21

See, I have inscribed you on the palms of My hands; Your walls are continually before me.
Isaiah 49:16

But now, thus says the LORD who created you, O Jacob, and He who formed you, O Israel: 'Fear not, for I have redeemed you; I have called you by your name; you are mine. When you pass through the waters, I will be with you; and through the rivers, they shall not overflow you. When you walk through the fire, you shall not be burned, nor shall the flame

185

scorch you. For I am the LORD your God, the Holy One of Israel, your Savior; I gave Egypt for your ransom, Ethiopia and Seba in your place. Since you were precious in My sight. You have been honored and I have loved you; Therefore I will give men for you, and people for your life. Fear not, for I am with you; I will bring your descendants from the east, and gather you from the west. I will say to the north, "Give them up!" and to the south, "Do not keep them back!" Bring My sons from afar, and My daughters from the ends of the earth— Everyone who is called by My name, whom I have created for My glory."   Isaiah 43:1-7

Many waters cannot quench love, nor can floods drown it. If a man would give for love all the wealth of his house, it would be utterly despised.   Song of Songs 8:7

"Even as the Evil One has plotted to keep you from My love, through trying to cause you to be 'swallowed up' in the earth, My love has reached you there. I have kept you through My love and I will continue to keep you. My Father sent His greatest treasure to earth to rescue you, My Bride, and I was also despised by My brothers," my King reminds me.

✿   ✿   ✿

*When the dragon saw that he had been hurled
down to the earth, he went in pursuit of the
woman who had given birth to the male child.
But the woman was given the two wings of the
great eagle, so that she could fly to her place in
the desert, where she is taken care of for a season and two seasons and half a season, away
from the serpent's presence. The serpent
spewed water like a river out of its mouth after
the woman, in order to sweep her away in the
flood; but the land came to her rescue — it
opened its mouth and swallowed up the river
which the dragon had spewed out of its mouth.
The dragon was infuriated over the woman
and went off to fight the rest of her children,
those who obey God's commands and bear witness to Yeshua.*   Revelation 12:13-17 (JNT)

*Because those whom he knew in advance, he
also determined in advance would be conformed to the pattern of his Son, so that he
might be the firstborn among many brothers;
and those whom he thus determined in advance, he also called; and those whom he
called, he also caused to be considered
righteous; and those whom he caused to be
considered righteous he also glorified! What,
then, are we to say to these things? If God is
for us, who can be against us? He who did not
spare even his own Son, but gave him up on
behalf of us all — is it possible that, having*

given us his Son, he would not give us every-
thing else too? So who will bring a charge
against God's chosen people? Certainly not
God — he is the one who causes them to be
considered righteous! Who punishes them?
Certainly not the Messiah Yeshua [Christ
Jesus], who died and more than that — has
been raised, is at the right hand of God and is
actually pleading on our behalf! Who will
separate us from the love of the Messiah?
Trouble? Hardship? Persecution? Hunger?
Poverty? Danger? War? ... For I am con-
vinced that neither death nor life, neither
angels nor other heavenly rulers, neither what
exists nor what is coming, neither powers
above nor powers below, nor any other created
thing will be able to separate us from the love
of God which comes to us through the Messiah
Yeshua, our Lord.

Romans 8:29-35 & 38-39 (JNT)

The LORD your God will raise up for you a
Prophet like me from your midst, from your
brethren. Him you shall hear, according to all
you desired of the LORD your God in Horeb
in the day of the assembly, saying, 'Let me not
hear again the voice of the LORD my God, nor
let me see this great fire anymore lest I die.'
And the LORD said to me 'What they have
spoken is good. I will raise up for them a
Prophet like you from among their brethren,

and will put My words in His mouth, and He shall speak to them all that I command Him. And it shall be that whoever will not hear My words, which He speaks in My name, I will require it of him.'   Deuteronomy 18:15-19

For He shall grow up before Him as a tender plant and as a root out of dry ground. He has no form [stately form] or comeliness [splendor]; And when we see Him there is no beauty [appearance] that we should desire Him. He is despised and rejected by men, a Man of sorrows and acquainted with grief. And we hid, as it were, our faces from Him: He was despised, and we did not esteem Him.

Isaiah 53:2-3

AUTHOR'S NOTE: The Bride spoke the words "draw me" in the first chapter of this book. The name *Moses* means "drawn out." Is Yeshua that prophet whom the LORD would raise up "from among your brethren" that would be greater than Moses? As the Bridegroom who draws the Bride to Himself, is He also the Messiah that is drawing Israel back to the land — not to replace Judah, but to take her place beside Judah, being joined together with Judah as a comfort and support, to strengthen them? As the Bride is being "drawn" to the Bridegroom, is Israel also being drawn to the Messiah? Could the verses from Revelation, quoted above, have a possible reference to the ten "lost tribes" of Israel that were seemingly "swallowed up in the earth?" Is the King saying that the waters and floods could not keep them from Him because the power of His love to draw them back was stronger than the power of the waters and floods?

We have a little sister, and she has no breasts. What shall we do for our sister in the day when she is spoken for?
Song of Songs 8:8

My feelings of fear and rejection melt away as I look upon my King's family and their city, Jerusalem. Compassion fills my heart and I long to comfort them. I begin speaking to Him of my concerns for them, saying, "What can we do for them? Their eyes were blinded to You for my sake, that I might be restored; therefore, only a remnant received You. But now, what of them in the day of Your power? Because of their rejection of You, their holy temple was taken away. They have suffered above all people and have not been able, for the most part, to receive the revelation of the fullness of Your love and the great future that You have planned for them. Therefore, they have not come to maturity. What can we do to defend our 'little sister' when bigger and stronger nations come against her — when they try to claim Jerusalem as their city?"

Woe to Ariel [Jerusalem], to Ariel, the city where David dwelt! ... You will be punished by the LORD of hosts with thunder and earthquake and great noise, with storm and tempest and the flame of devouring fire. The multitude of all the nations who fight against Ariel, even all who fight against her and her fortress, and distress her, shall be as a dream of a night vision. It shall even be as when a hungry man dreams, and look — he eats; but when he awakes, and his soul is still empty; Or as when a thirsty man dreams, and look — he drinks; But he awakes and indeed he is faint, and his soul still craves: So the multitude of all the nations shall be, who fight against Mount Zion." Pause and wonder! Blind yourselves and be blind! They are drunk, but not with wine; they stagger, but not with intoxicating drink. For the LORD has poured out on you the spirit of deep sleep, and has closed your eyes, namely, the prophets; and He has covered your heads, namely, the seers. The whole vision has become to you like the words of a book [scroll] that is sealed, which men deliver to one who is literate, saying, "Read this, please"; and he says, "I cannot, for it is sealed." Then the book is

delivered to one who is illiterate [does not know books] saying "Read this, please"; and he says "I am not literate." Therefore the LORD said: "Inasmuch as these people draw near to Me with their mouths and honor Me with their lips, but have removed their hearts far from Me, and their fear toward Me is taught by the commandment of men, therefore, behold, I will again do a marvelous work among this people, a marvelous work and a wonder; for the wisdom of their wise men shall perish, and the understanding of their prudent men shall be hidden." ... Is it not yet a very little while till Lebanon shall be turned into a fruitful field, and the fruitful field be esteemed as a forest? In that day the deaf shall hear the words of the book, and the eyes of the blind shall see out of obscurity and out of darkness. The humble also shall increase their joy in the LORD, and the poor among men shall rejoice in the Holy One of Israel.

Isaiah 29:1, 6-14 & 17-19

If she is a wall, we will build upon her a battlement of silver; and if she is a door, we will enclose her with boards of cedar.

Song of Songs 8:9

"If she is willing to be joined with us, we will add

our family to hers. We will build up and fortify Jerusalem as her redeemed children return and become as a wall of praise surrounding her.

"If she is open to receive us, we, the army of those who are returning to our roots, will come in and become a strength and support to her."

For Zion's sake I will not hold my peace,
And for Jerusalem's sake I will not rest,
Until the righteousness goes forth as brightness,
And her salvation as a lamp that burns.
The Gentiles shall see your righteousness,
And all kings your glory. ...
You shall no longer be termed Forsaken,
Nor shall your land any more be termed Desolate;
But you shall be called Hephzibah, [My delight is in her], and your land Beulah [married];
For the Lord delights in you,
And your land shall be married.
For as a young man marries a virgin,
So shall your sons marry you;
And as the bridegroom rejoices over the bride,
So shall your God rejoice over you.
I have set watchmen on your walls, O Jerusalem,
Who shall never hold their peace day or night.

You who make mention of the LORD, do not
keep silent,
And give Him no rest, till He establishes,
And till He makes Jerusalem a praise in the
earth. ...
Indeed, the LORD hath proclaimed
To the end of the world:
"Say to the daughter of Zion,
'Surely your salvation is coming;
Behold, His reward is with Him,
And His work before Him.' "
And they shall call them, The Holy People,
The Redeemed of the LORD;
And you shall be called, Sought Out, A City
Not Forsaken.   Isaiah 62:1-2, 4-7 &11-12

AUTHOR'S NOTE: The Hebrew word for *wall* is taken from a root word meaning "to join; a wall of protection." (SC #2346) The Hebrew word for *door* is taken from a root word meaning "to dangle, i.e. to let down a bucket (for drawing out water; figurative, to deliver; draw (out), lift up." It is taken from another root word meaning "to slacken, or be feeble; figuratively, to be oppressed; bring low, be not equal, etc." (SC #1817 from #1803, from #1809) The word *build* is taken from a Hebrew word meaning "to build (literally and figuratively), (begin to) obtain children, make repair, etc." (SC #1129)

194

I am a wall, and my breasts like towers;
then I became in his eyes as one who
found peace. Song of Songs 8:10

Joined together with the other daughters of Jerusalem, we are as an invincible fortress against the Evil One. Our unity has brought abundant health and strength to our city. Therefore, we dwell together in great prosperity and peace.

Therefore He shall give them up, until the time
that she who is in labor has given birth; then
the remnant of His brethren shall return to the
children of Israel. And He shall stand and feed
His flock in the strength of the LORD, in the
majesty of the name of the LORD His God;
and they shall abide, and now He shall be great
to the ends of the earth; and this One shall be
peace. Micah 5:3-5

"Or let him take hold of My strength,
That he may make peace with Me;
And he shall make peace with Me."
Those who come He shall cause to take root in
Jacob;
Israel shall blossom and bud,

195

And fill the face of the world with fruit.
Isaiah 27:5-6

Rejoice with Jerusalem, and be glad with her, all you who love her; Rejoice for joy with her, all you who mourn for her; that you may feed and be satisfied with the consolation of her bosom, that you may drink deeply and be delighted with the abundance of her glory.
Isaiah 66:10-11

Pray for the peace of Jerusalem: May they prosper who love you. Peace be within your walls, prosperity within your palaces. For the sake of my brethren and companions, I will now say, Peace be within you. Because of the house of the Lord our God I will seek your good.
Psalm 122:6-8

How beautiful upon the mountains are the feet of him who brings good news, who proclaims peace, who brings glad tidings of good things, who proclaims salvation, who says to Zion, "Your God reigns!" Your watchmen shall lift up their voices, with their voices they shall sing together; for they shall see eye to eye when the LORD brings back Zion. Break forth into joy, sing together, you waste places of Jerusalem! For the LORD has comforted His people, He has redeemed Jerusalem. The LORD has made bare His holy arm in the eyes of all the nations; and all the ends of the earth shall see the salvation of our God.   Isaiah 52:7-10

I do not pray for these alone, but also for those who will believe in Me through their word; that they may all be one, as You, Father, are in Me, and I in You; that they also may be one in Us, that the world may believe that You sent Me. And the glory which You gave Me I have given them, that they may be one, just as We are one; I in them, and You in Me; that they may be made perfect in one, that the world may know that You have sent Me, and have loved them as you have loved Me.   John 17:20-23

Therefore remember that you, once Gentiles in the flesh who are called Uncircumcision by what is called the Circumcision made in the flesh by hands — that at that time you were without Christ, being aliens from the common-wealth of Israel and strangers from the convenants of promise, having no hope and without God in the world. But now in Christ Jesus you who once were far off have been made near by the blood of Christ. For He him-self is our peace, who has made both one, and has broken down the middle wall of division between us, having abolished in His flesh the enmity, that is, the law of commandments con-tained in ordinances, so as to create in Himself one new man from the two, thus making peace,

and that He might reconcile them both to God in one body through the cross, thereby putting to death the enmity. And He came and preached peace to you who were afar off and to those who were near. For through Him we both have access by one Spirit to the Father. Now, therefore, you are no longer strangers and foreigners, but fellow citizens with the saints and members of the household of God, having been built on the foundation of the apostles and prophets, Jesus Christ Himself being the chief cornerstone, in whom the whole building, being joined together, grows into a holy temple in the Lord, in whom you also are being built together for a habitation of God in the Spirit. Ephesians 2:11-22
(Also see Ephesians 4:1-6 & 13)

And all these, having obtained a good testimony through faith, did not receive the promise, God having provided something better for us, that they should not be made perfect apart from us. Hebrews 11:39-40

Author's Note: The word *perfect* in the above verse is taken from a Greek word meaning "to complete, i.e. accomplish, or consummate." It is taken from a root word meaning "to set out for a definite point or goal, the point aimed at as a limit, i.e. the conclusion of an act or state, termination, result, purpose, etc." (SC #5048, from

#5046, from #5056) The Hebrew word for *peace* is taken from a root word meaning "safe, well, happy, friendly; also welfare, i.e. health, prosperity, peace, etc. - to be safe (in mind, body or estate; to be friendly: - make amends ... make restutution, restore, etc." (SC #7965 from #7999)

Solomon had a vineyard at Baal Hamon; He leased the vineyard to keepers; Everyone was to bring for its fruit a thousand pieces of silver.   Song of Songs 8:11

The King of Peace planted His garden in a place where He had been made Lord over a multitude. After planting His vine, He left it in the care of overseers and expected to receive much increase from His planting. Everyone that lived by the fruit of this vine should bring to the King of Peace a hundredfold increase.

Now listen to another parable. There was a farmer who planted a vineyard. He put a wall around it, dug a pit for the winepress and built a tower, then he rented it to tenants and left. When the harvest-time came, he sent his servants to the tenants to collect his share of the crop. But the tenants seized his servants —

this one they beat up, that one they killed, an-other they stoned. So he sent some other servants, more than the first group, and they did the same to them. Finally, he sent them his son, saying, "My son they will respect." But when the tenants saw the son, they said to each other, "This is the heir. Come, let's kill him and take his inheritance!" So they grabbed him, threw him out of the vineyard and killed him. Now when the owner of the vineyard comes, what will he do to those tenants? They answered him, "He will viciously destroy those vicious men and rent out the vineyard to other tenants who will give him his share of the crop when it's due." Yeshua [Jesus] said to them, "Haven't you ever read in the Tanakh [Old Testament], 'The very rock which the builders rejected has become the cornerstone! This has come from Adonai [the Lord], and in our eyes it is amazing?' (Psalm 118:22-23) Therefore, I tell you that the Kingdom of God will be taken away from you and given to the kind of people that will produce its fruit."

Mattityahu (Matthew) 21:33-43 (JNT)

My own vineyard is before me. You, O So-lomon, may have a thousand, and those who keep its fruit two hundred.

Song of Songs 8:12

200

"How wonderful it is to be restored to my own vineyard, my King! I gladly bring to You all the fruit which my life has produced since You called me to become Your Bride, for it is only through the life that You have given to me as Your Bride that I have become fruitful.

"But I would like to also give an offering to the ones who have remained in the vineyard while I was yet an outcast. They also should be rewarded, for they were the keepers of the word through which I heard Your Love Song. And it was from them that You descended. It is through them and their rejection of You that I have received my riches as Your Bride. They didn't realize what they were doing, because their eyes had been blinded for my sake, until you came and found me and restored me to Your fold. They have also shed their blood to regain Your city and to hold it until our return."

"In that day," says the LORD, "I will assemble the lame, I will gather the outcast and those whom I have afflicted; I will make the lame a remnant, and the outcast a strong nation; So the LORD will reign over them in Mount Zion from now on, even forever. And you, O tower of the flock, the stronghold of the daughter of Zion, to you shall it come, even the former dominion shall come, the kingdom of the daughter of Jerusalem. Micah 4:6-8

But now I am going to Yerushalayim [Jerusalem] with aid for God's people there. For Macedonia and Achaia thought it would be good to make some contribution to the poor among God's people in Yerushalayim. They were pleased to do it, but the fact is that they owe it to them. For if the Gentiles have shared with the Jews in spiritual matters, then the Gentiles clearly have a duty to help the Jews in material matters. So when I have finished this task and made certain that they have received this fruit ... . Romans 15:25-28 (JNT)

However, what was sown on rich soil is the one who hears the message and understands it; such a person will surely bear fruit, a hundred or sixty or thirty times what was sown.
Mattityahu (Matthew) 13:23 (JNT)

Also, O Judah, a harvest is appointed for you, when I return the captives of My people.
Hosea 6:11

AUTHOR'S NOTE: Could the thousand pieces of silver represent the one hundredfold increase of the ten tribes of Ephraim? If so, the two hundred pieces given to the keepers of the vineyard could then represent the increase belonging to the two tribes of Judah.

You who dwell in the gardens, the com-panions listen for your voice — Let me hear it!   Song of Songs 8:13

Even as I began my journey by hearing the love song and being drawn to the Singer by the sweet-ness that was to be heard, both in His words and in the melody of the refrain, now the King encourages me to sing forth my song of love back to Him — proclaiming it openly, even loudly — so that my companions in the garden may hear it and be drawn.

My King is also drawn to me when He hears my love song to Him. He is moved when He hears His Bride crying out to see His face. The 'Love Song' draws Him to His Bride even as His Bride is drawn to Him when she hears it.

"Now that you are dwelling together in the gar-dens, the daughters of Jerusalem are ready to hear your voice. As they hear you sing your love song to Me, they will be moved to jealousy because of your intimate relationship with Me, and they will to be drawn nearer to Me," my King encourages me.

"Then they will join with you, My Bride, and to-gether the whole House of Israel, with one voice, will sing the song that I have waited to hear."

And I will pour on the house of David and on the inhabitants of Jerusalem the Spirit of grace and supplication; then they will look on Me whom they have pierced; they will mourn for Him as one mourns for his only son, and grieve for Him as one grieves for a firstborn.
Zechariah 12:10

Then those who feared the LORD spoke to one another, and the LORD listened and heard them; So a book of remembrance was written before Him for those who fear the LORD and who meditate on [esteem] His name. "They shall be Mine," says the LORD of hosts, "On the day that I make them My jewels. And I will spare them as a man spares his own son who serves him." Malachi 3:16-17

AUTHOR'S NOTE: The Hebrew word for *companions* is taken from a root word meaning "to join, be compact, couple (together), have fellowship with, heap up, join (self together), also an associate: - knit together." (SC #2269, from #2266 and #2270)

Make haste, my beloved, and be like a gazelle or young stag on the mountains of spices. Song of Songs 8:14

"With 'one voice,' with all the longing in our heart, with our whole being, we cry out to our King, 'Come, Messiah! Please, do not delay! In all Your beauty and grace, come! In all the power of Your anointing, come! Come quickly, for Your Bride has prepared herself and awaits Your coming, O Bridegroom!' "

Yerushalayim! Yerushalayim! You kill the prophets! You stone those who are sent to you! How often I wanted to gather your children, just as a hen gathers her chickens under her wings, but you refused! Look! God is abandoning your house to you, leaving it desolate. For I tell you, from now on, you will not see me again until you say, "Blessed is he who comes in the name of the Adonai."
Mattityahu (Matthew) 23:37-39 (JNT)
(From Jeremiah 22:5 & Psalm 118:26)

I, Yeshua, have sent my angel to give you this testimony for the Messianic communities. I am the Root and Offspring of David, the bright Morning Star. The Spirit and the Bride say, "Come!" Let anyone who hears say "Come!" And let anyone who is thirsty come — let anyone who wishes, take the water of life free of charge. Revelation 22:16-17 (JNT)

The one who is testifying to these things says, "Yes, I am coming soon!" Amen! Come, Lord Yeshua! Revelation 22:20 (JNT)

Questions, Chapter Eight

1. Why does the bride wish that her Beloved was more like her brother? (verse 1)
2. Is there a reason for "the charge" being placed in this specific spot? (verse 4)
3. Who is asking the question, "Who is this coming up from the wilderness, leaning upon her Beloved?" (verse 5)
4. Who is the one who was "awakened under the apple tree?" (verse 5)
5. What is the bride's response to her fear? (verse 6)
6. Who is the little sister who has "no breasts?" (verse 8)
7. What is the plan to help her? (verse 9)
8. What is the meaning of a vineyard at Baal Hamon? (verse 11)
9. Who are "the companions that listen for Your voice?" (verse 13)

Give ear, O Shepherd of Israel,
You who lead Joseph like a flock;
You who dwell between the cherubim, shine forth!
Before Ephraim, Benjamin and Manasseh,
Stir up Your strength,
And come and save us!
Restore us [turn us again, KJV], O God;
Cause Your face to shine,
And we shall be saved!
Return, we beseech You, O God of hosts;
Look down from heaven and see,
And visit this vine
And the vineyard which Your right hand has planted,
And the branch that You made strong for Yourself.
Let Your hand be upon the man of Your right hand,
Upon the son of man whom You made strong for Yourself.
Then we will not turn back from You;
Revive us, and we will call upon Your name.
Restore us [turn us again, KJV], O Lord God of hosts;
Cause Your face to shine,
And we shall be saved!

Psalm 80:1-3 , 14-15 & 17-19

Bibliography

Brown, Michael L. *Our Hands Are Stained With Blood*. (Shippensburg, PA: Destiny Image, 1992)

Coxon, Dr. DeWayne. *Living Prophecies — A Crumbling Wall Between Christians and Jews*. (Cedar Springs, MI: Blossoming Rose, 1992)

Doron, Reuven. *One New Man*. (Cedar Rapids, IA: Embrace, 1993)

Eckstein, Rabbi Yechiel. *What Christians Should Know About Jews and Judaism*. (Waco, TX: Word Books, 1984)

Guyon, Madam. *The Song of Songs*. (Augusta, Maine: Christian Books Publishing House, 1984).

Lash, Jamie. *A Kiss A Day*. (Hagerstown, MD: EBED Publications, 1996)

Nee, Watchman. *Song of Songs*. (Fort Washington, PA: Christian Literature Crusade, 1965)

Penn-Lewis, Jessie. *Thy Hidden Ones*. (Bournemouth, Hants, England: The Overcomer Book Room, 1951).

Scherman, Rabbi N. and Zlotowitz, Rabbi Meir, Editors. *Shir ha Shirim*. [The ArtScroll Tanach Series] (Brooklyn, NY: Mesorah Publications, Ltd., 1977).

Taylor, Wade E. *The Secret of the Stairs.* (Hagerstown, MD: EBED Publications, 1996)

Weiner, Bob & Rose. *Bible Studies for the Preparation of the Bride.* (Gainesville, FL: Maranatha Publications, 1980).

Wooten, Batya Ruth. *In Search of Israel.* (Shippensburg, PA: Destiny Image, 1988)